SMART
TIME INVESTMENT
FOR **BUSINESS**

128 ways the best in business use their time

KATE CHRISTIE

'Business owners – all of us – need more time. We are busy! Often we wear way too many hats, work way too many hours, and worry way too much about everything we have on our plates. It is a constant juggle. Ironically, the vast number of business owners started on this journey because we wanted control over our time and over our own destiny – we wanted time to spend with our families, our partners, our children, our friends, to travel and to explore our many interests. So what happened? Well, no-one taught us how to invest our time. We lost the "off" switch. Kate Christie is a time management expert. She has delivered another great book – her third – this time to specifically help business owners invest their time with intent to generate the greatest possible return. I absolutely recommend this book to all business owners – because it's time to take back control.'

Andrew Griffiths, International Bestselling Author and Global Entrepreneurial Speaker

'Kate has an innate way of getting into your head to make positive change. Time is our most precious commodity; master it and you can be a business owner that achieves a lot more than most. This book is a must read for those that dare to get real about where they spend their time.'

Bree James, Publisher

'As a business that promotes flexibility and work/life balance for working mums, we weren't really "walking our own talk" at JustMums Recruitment and desperately needed to make changes in the way we managed our time. After working closely with Kate Christie now for over a year, we are thrilled to have learnt so much to help keep us focused on what we, as business owners, should spend our time on and what we shouldn't waste our time on (or should outsource). Kate's coaching has helped our business regain control of our time; we have expanded our team and business interests; and we have set some pretty ambitious goals for the future. You will love this book – *SMART Time Investment for Business*.'

Erin Kefalas and Rachel Perkins, JustMums Recruitment

'One thing we identified in our team was that time allocation on specific tasks varies from person to person, even those doing the same role. Recognising we are all different and respond in different ways is important for any diverse team, and Kate's concepts provide something for every single person no matter where they are on the continuum of time management skill. Her simple and real-life examples coupled with practical applications provide a takeaway for everybody.'

Dwain Richardson, Managing Director, Corporate Challenge Events

'Kate Christie's *SMART Time Investment for Business* is jam-packed full of brilliant strategies to be more productive in business. Her practical, easy-to-read writing style enables you to take action quickly to get results immediately.'

Amanda Fisher, The Cash Flow Queen

'Productivity Perfection! Kate Christie provides an amazing suite of "Time Investment" strategies for those in business in a no-nonsense, direct, practical, and easy-to-implement style. Having seen Kate speak on SMART Time Investment a number of times, her written voice is authentic. As a business woman, I have founded, grown and sold one business and now work globally with my second business, so I know first hand that time really is of the essence. I have the feeling I will continue to carry Kate's book with me as my go-to TIME resource.'

Katrina McCarter, Founder & CEO, Marketing To Mums

'Kate's message is powerful – we all have the same amount of time. As business people, we choose a path that allows us growth, freedom of choice and infinite opportunity to design our own destiny. Every single day, every single one of us wakes up with the same number of hours in the day. Using our time wisely makes a difference to the lives we live, and Kate's strategies will make this a much easier proposition. I know I will get more done and reach greater heights by applying the wisdom in this book.'

Anoushka Gungadin, CEO & Founder: Global CQ, Vice-President: Australia India Business Council, Victoria, Speaker, Best-selling Author

'Kate's time management strategies are a godsend. As someone who works with small business owners, start-ups and entrepreneurs all the time, I know how time-poor they can be if they are not organised. With this book there are no excuses as to why things aren't getting done. I would recommend Kate's book to any small business owner that wants to have some organisational and time-saving strategies to hand. By following Kate's process, I have managed to free up a lot more time than I ever had in the past!'

Jules Brooke, Founder, Handle Your Own PR

'Thanks to working with Kate we now have daily practices in place that have improved the entire organisation's intelligence around time management, time blocking, setting big hairy tasks to start the day, and reducing the occurrences of multitasking. This has led to an enhanced respect for each other's time – moreover, our team are more often problem solving for themselves due to a delay in "interrupting" each other and the heightened awareness and respect we all have for each others' time and focus. The lessons we learnt as a business have certainly helped positively drive our ability to service more clients to succeed on their property planning journey. Time is our most precious commodity – thank you Kate for your wonderful education.'

David Johnston, Managing Director, Property Planning Australia

'Kate's approach to time investment is refreshingly honest. As a business owner, it's hard to see how we can get more hours in our day but this book manages to achieve it. Kate's advice is direct, practical and serves as a helpful reminder that consistency and commitment are key. I love the idea that I can re-read these pages as my business matures and new strategies are needed. This book is a great tool for any time-poor business owner.'

Claire Pales, Author of *The Secure CIO*, Director 27 Lanterns Pty Ltd

Dedication

To my three for making me get up and on
with it every single day – you are Ace.

Project management and text design by Michael Hanrahan Publishing
Cover design by Peter Reardon

Contents

Foreword by David Koch **xv**

Introduction **1**

About This Book **7**

128 WAYS THE BEST IN BUSINESS USE THEIR TIME

1. Don't Waste Your Time **13**
2. Time Investment Versus Time Management **14**
3. Choice **15**
4. Productivity Versus Efficiency **16**
5. Don't Be Busy **17**
6. Find A Gap **18**
7. Be Courageous **23**
8. What Type Of Business Are You Running? **25**
9. Think Like An Athlete **26**
10. Business With Passion **28**
11. Business With Purpose **31**
12. Leverage All Of Your Skills **34**
13. Hustle Until You Can Almost Afford Not To **37**
14. You Must Have Grit **40**
15. Set Audacious Goals **44**
16. Write A Business Plan **48**
17. Undertake Regular Business Styling **50**
18. Too Old? Rubbish **51**
19. (Hourly) Rate Yourself **53**
20. Is This The *Best* Use Of My Time? **55**
21. Financial Cost **56**

22. Opportunity Cost **58**
23. Emotional Cost **59**
24. Physical Cost **60**
25. Saying No **61**
26. Set Boundaries For Yourself **64**
27. Embrace Processes **64**
28. Leverage Technology **67**
29. The 5 SMART Steps **68**
30. Being Self-Aware **69**
31. Map Your Time **73**
32. Analyse Your Time **74**
33. Reframe **76**
34. Take Control **76**
35. Conduct An Annual Detox **77**
36. Lock In Me Time **78**
37. Repetition And Ritual **80**
38. Think Outside The Square **81**
39. Outsource As Soon As You Possibly Can **82**
40. Focus On Your Strengths And Outsource Your Weaknesses **85**
41. Business Outsourcing **88**
42. 50 Jobs You Can Outsource In Your Business **89**
43. Home Outsourcing **92**
44. 50 Jobs You Can Outsource At Home **96**
45. Get A Cleaner **99**
46. Don't Clean **100**
47. Smart Outsourcing **100**
48. Insourcing At Home **103**
49. 50 Jobs You Can Insource At Home **106**
50. A Half Hour Of Power **112**
51. Shop Online **113**

52.   Rejects **113**
53.   Deal With The Total Rejects **115**
54.   Create A 'Don't-Do List' **116**
55.   Reject Guilt **118**
56.   Deal With The Partial Rejects **120**
57.   Reject Fridge Gazing **121**
58.   Reject Peak Hour **122**
59.   Reject Ironing **123**
60.   Reject Piling **123**
61.   Work/Life Integration **124**
62.   Free Up Space In Your Brain **126**
63.   Manage Your Passwords **127**
64.   Reject Perfectionism **128**
65.   Evaluate Your Decisions **130**
66.   Make (Simple) Decisions Fast **130**
67.   Make (Simple) Decisions Once **132**
68.   Make (Complex) Decisions Slowly **132**
69.   Create A Great Morning Routine **134**
70.   Piggy Back Good Habits **135**
71.   Respond Don't React **136**
72.   Define Success Early **137**
73.   Test And Measure **139**
74.   Perseverance And Resilience **141**
75.   Fail Fast **145**
76.   Learn, Unlearn, Then Learn Some More **146**
77.   Invest In Learning **150**
78.   Embrace Keyboard Shortcuts **152**
79.   Surround Yourself With The Right People **152**
80.   Find The Right Business Mentors **153**
81.   Find Your Posse **157**
82.   Learn From Big Business **160**

83. Create Business Protocols **161**
84. Create Time Budgets **162**
85. Understand Parkinson's Law **163**
86. Set Realistic, Non-Negotiable Deadlines **165**
87. Leverage Parkinson's Law **165**
88. Set A Timer **166**
89. Break It Down With Mind Maps **167**
90. Plan **168**
91. Active Vs Reactive Mindset **169**
92. To-Do Lists **170**
93. SMART To-Do List Process **172**
94. How To Identify Your Key Tasks **174**
95. Emptying Your Too-Hard Basket **175**
96. Calendar Basics **176**
97. Colour Code Your Calendar **177**
98. Create An Annual Calendar **182**
99. Use A Cloud Calendar **184**
100. Batch Similar Tasks **184**
101. Batch Your Energy **185**
102. Batch Your High Energy **187**
103. Batch Your Low Energy **188**
104. Batch A Buffer **189**
105. Control Your Device Usage **190**
106. Batch Emails **192**
107. Batch Social Media **194**
108. Batch Some More **195**
109. An Hour Of Power **196**
110. Take A Break **197**
111. Triage Your Emails **198**
112. Use Action-Led Email Subjects **201**
113. Control Your Calls **202**

114. Get Smart With Voicemail **203**

115. Embrace Texting **204**

116. Leave Smart Messages **205**

117. Use Your Lost Time **205**

118. Use Your Commute **208**

119. Control Meetings **209**

120. Multitasking Versus Single Focus **211**

121. Multitasking At Home **212**

122. Slow Cook **213**

123. Switch On And Off **214**

124. Control Interruptions **215**

125. Allow Urgent Interruptions **217**

126. Create A Parking List **217**

127. Own Your Success **219**

128. Just Start **222**

Thank You **227**

About Kate Christie **228**

About Time Stylers **229**

FOREWORD

The business owners I speak to regularly cite time management as the number one key challenge they face in their business. And it's true – business owners are often time poor; jacks of all trades; juggling multiple competing priorities; rushing from one task to the next; with an ever-present sense of overwhelm; constantly putting out fires.

As a small business owner myself, as well as juggling my media commitments, I was immediately struck by Kate Christie's third book *SMART Time Investment for Business*. Kate has delivered a practical, punchy book full of productivity strategies written specifically for business owners. She punctuates her productivity advice with anecdotes and stories from some truly amazing and inspirational business owners from around the world, who share how they use time to their advantage, as well as the lessons they have learnt along their own business journeys.

As a finance commentator, I particularly enjoy how Kate has reframed the negative concept of *Time Management* to embrace and champion a mindset of *Time Investment* – where she encourages you, as a business owner, to think about, treat and utilise your time in the same way as you do your money.

We all know that money is a precious, enormously valuable, and limited resource that you need to consciously invest for the greatest possible return so that your wealth and success grows. It's time to think about your Time the same way.

I highly recommend *SMART Time Investment for Business* to all business owners and entrepreneurs – take control of your time and live your greatest possible life.

David Koch, Media commentator and Chairman, Pinstripe Media

Introduction

Having It All

Back in the Olden Days, which my children refer to as any time south of the year 2000, I was one of a generation who was told that I could *have it all.*

My parents were born as World War II ended, went to the (free) local primary school and the (free) local high school, the latter of which ended at year 10. They then travelled to the city for the (free) year 11 and the (free) year 12 and, as they were lucky enough to not have to get jobs straight from school to help support their parents' incomes, they went to (free) university. Their parents, my grandparents, were strictly confined to the working class, and had lived – and in some cases fought – through World War I and World War II. They never had the luxury to dream big.

This can only have constrained my parents. They were the first in their families to get a university education, and they both became teachers, which was pretty much as big as you could dream growing up working class in post-war Australia. They survived the '60s, voted labor, lived on the wrong side of the river, and, once they became parents, sent their three daughters to the same (free) local primary school they went to.

Freedom And Space And Options

But that is where the similarities end. Because they dreamed big for their girls – very big.

I was a child of the 1970s: flared jeans; shoes with smiley faces on them; loads of velour; and big-collared shirts. I grew up in a different world to my parents (no world war for one), and very different from my own children (no technology, no devices, no uber-connectedness). I had a phenomenal amount of freedom compared to my parents, and a very different, innocent, wholesome and basic kind of freedom compared to my kids. Without 800 online friends, my cohort was entirely made up of the kids in my immediate neighbourhood, who would dare each other to nick 20 cents from their mums' bags so that we could dink each other on our bikes down to the local milk bar, without helmets, to buy paper bags stuffed full of lollies, which we would gorge on the ride back, riding hands free.

Freedom and space and options.

From as early as I can remember I was told that I could do or be *anything* I wanted. The possibilities were only limited by my imagination, my guts and my drive. When I expressed an interest in working internationally at the age of 16, my dad encouraged me to write a letter (no computers, no emails) to the United Nations asking about summer internships. I don't think I ever received a reply, and god only knows how I was going to manage the commute, but that wasn't the point. My sister was in love with the Six Million Dollar Man – *write him a letter*, my parents said. Unlike the UN, he wrote back.

That was the way we were raised. Want it? *Go and get it.*

My simple formula for success back then was hard work plus a massive amount of drive plus a modicum of talent plus an earnest desire to make my parents proud, and I could pretty much have it all. And it worked.

Living The Dream ... ?

That all changed in the year 2000, when we clicked over from the Olden Days to modern times and I had three babies in three-and-a-half years. But hell, I didn't let that stop me ... initially, at least.

No-one could run faster in high heels than me to pick the kids up from child care before 6 pm when time and money became confused and the creche would start charging $20 for each minute a parent was late; throw the kids in the car; play loud music and sing in that frenetic kind of way you do when you have three small, hangry children crying in the back seat of your car; stop at the supermarket for essentials – nappies and wine; shove a peanut-butter sandwich at the starving minions to tide them over while preparing a proper dinner; check my emails; feed the kids; check my emails; bath the kids; check my emails; manage the whole PJs–teeth–books routine; drink my third glass of wine; check my emails; wave at my husband as he arrives home; check my emails; fall into bed ... and check my emails.

I was living the dream.

Something had to give, and it did – big time. It was a Monday morning, and – wanting to be a super-parent along with being a super-woman generally – I delayed my departure for work so that I could drop my son at school. There I was, in my beautiful black suit, red lipstick, high heels, and with a small child clinging to me in hysterics because it was *cupcake day*. Of course it was. I don't know who comes up with these ideas – it certainly isn't working parents. Clearly, I did not have any cupcakes. I must have missed the memo.

Later, radiating guilt and covered in my son's snot and thinking about the 25 years of therapy my son would need to get over the cupcake debacle, I rushed (late) into the already full boardroom at work. It took me a few seconds to register that the room was silent (maybe it was the snot). Everyone around the table looked at me and then at their watches, and then resumed the meeting. And I had the profound realisation that I was the only member of the executive leadership team who didn't have a full-time wife.

Thunderbolt.

Not long after, I resigned from the job that I loved, that I was great at, and that gave me an enormous amount of self-worth, because I felt I had no other option. I had backed myself into a corner. I had two choices, I told myself: be a great mum, or have a great career.

What on earth had happened to the promise that I could *have it all*? I felt cheated, lied to, exhausted, set up, and a complete failure who, having tried to fly the flag, had in fact dismally let the sisterhood down.

Finding Time

But I was wrong. I *did* have other options. If only I knew then what I know now about TIME.

TIME is now my passion – I am a Time Investment expert, and I am in the business of helping you find time. Lots of time.

I work with high-performing business owners and entrepreneurs to teach them the frameworks, strategies and mindset to maximise their productivity (across all aspects of their lives) to take their success to the next level and to absolutely ensure that they never, ever feel their only option is to opt out of doing what they love.

I have gathered around me a posse of driven, intelligent, determined and overwhelmingly incredible business people who inspire me every day. And by surrounding myself with these individuals, I get more done, I reach greater heights, and in turn I give generously to their growth. It's all about working together to push each one of us higher to achieve more than we could alone.

For me, it all starts with how you invest your TIME.

I believe that you are extraordinary. When you gain control of your time you will be unstoppable.

Come and join my posse and learn from, share with, and be one of the best in business.

Kate x

About This Book

You started your business because you had a brilliant idea for a product or service that solved the problems of a niche market that you love working with. But there is more to it than that. You are a high achiever. You are a risk taker. You value your freedom. You thrive on being your own boss. You want to create for yourself and your family a lifestyle that you love.

And yet, we live in the Age of Information, which means we also live in the Age of Distraction – we are constantly switched on and constantly accessible. Never before have we been so busy, so stressed and so time poor.

The Three Biggest Time Challenges For Business Owners

As a business owner there are three key time investment challenges you face:

1. You don't have enough time.
2. You don't control the time you have.
3. You don't focus on the right tasks at the right time.

This book is designed to help you overcome these three, and many more, time challenges so that you can invest your time with intent for your greatest possible success.

We are all creatures of habit – the way in which you manage today will generally be the same as you managed your day yesterday, last week, last year … but not from tomorrow. From tomorrow, you will have a new mindset on how you invest your time. Why would you wait and waste even *more* time?

Central to changing your bad time habits is to clearly identify which of your current habits and behaviours impact your ability to invest your time well. These are the habits to discard in favour of better habits and behaviours that allow you to focus on the right tasks at the right time to produce sustained excellent results.

Getting The Most Out Of This Book

This is not a *time management* book, it is a *time investment* book. It contains 128 proven time investment strategies to help you power up your productivity. The strategies are short, sharp, practical and direct – I'm not here to waste your time. The strategies are not provided in any particular order, however some strategies do couple well, and logically can be implemented together – look for **highlighted words throughout** the book that indicate there is another strategy in the book you should consider implementing at the same time. This will also include the relevant strategy number, so you can save time and go directly to the strategy you are looking for.

Not every one of the 128 strategies will work for you, your business model or your personal style, so here's how to get the most out of this book:

1. Read this book with a pen and pad of sticky notes in hand. Identify your quick wins first – the low-hanging fruit – those strategies that sound simple, easy to implement and maintain, and which seem so obviously worthwhile to you that you can't believe you haven't used them before. Flag these as a priority to implement immediately.

2. Next, move to the strategies that resonate with you but which you know will be more challenging for you to successfully implement.

3. For each productivity strategy you implement, note the ways you can use the strategy so that you can best test and measure its effectiveness. Use a time tracker to track the amount of time you reclaim (you can access the Time Stylers free time tracker at www.timestylers.com), and for every hour you reclaim, lock a 'Want' into your calendar (and make sure you turn up).

4. Some of the strategies at first glance might appear to be contradictory – they aren't, it's more that different strategies will best suit different scenarios.

5. Reject the strategies that simply don't resonate with you – don't waste your time. In a year or so when you revisit this book, some of the previously rejected strategies might make more sense for you – but only you can make this decision.

There are a number of key themes repeated throughout the book – that's because they are important, and the act of repetition will help them stick. **Repetition and ritual (37)** are key to creating and sustaining good new time habits (or habits of any kind). You'll also find throughout the book contributions from leading business figures and entrepreneurs, including their stories about how they have used some of the time investment strategies in this book to boost their business and personal lives.

The act of finding and then harnessing your lost time will take commitment, discipline and personal accountability. There is no magic bullet – you will need to invest some of your time to identify your poor time habits, consider better time habits, and then implement the new habits with **repetition and ritual (37)**.

You have nothing to lose except your poor time habits. What you will regain is hours of time to do what you love: more time with your family and friends, more time to spend on your own health and wellbeing, and more time to strategically build the next stage of your business success.

And isn't that why you started your business in the first place?

So, let's get started!

> *'I just want to use my time wisely to become the best version of myself.'*
>
> **June Sarpong**, MBE

128 ways the best in business use their time

Don't Waste Your Time

As a business owner, there are many ways you can lose time. You can:

- squander it
- waste it
- kill it
- blow it
- fail to control it
- spin it.

And then you can also:

- procrastinate
- sweat the small stuff
- fail to prioritise
- focus on the wrong tasks at the wrong time.

For the purposes of each strategy in this book, the above time-killing concepts are lumped together into the general expression *a waste of time*.

Bottom line – stop doing it.

☑ Write down three ways you could use this strategy:

1. _____
2. _____
3. _____

☐ This strategy is a priority for me.
☐ I have implemented this strategy.

Time Investment Versus Time Management

The great irony about time management is how much time we spend thinking about how we could, or should, be managing our time differently to get more done.

Was there ever a greater **waste of time (1)**? Probably not.

Happily, the concept of time management is one you can move away from right now, forever, because there is a better way.

Time management is an outdated concept.

Time is the one asset we all have exactly the same amount of, and which no-one can gain more of, no matter how clever, wealthy or stealthy they are. As such, the smart workaround is to learn how to think about, treat and utilise your time in such a way as to ensure that you use all of it well, all of the time.

Smart business owners think about their time differently because they can't afford to do otherwise. Move away from a mindset of having to *manage your time* to a mindset of wanting to *invest your time.* Start thinking about your time the way you think about your money – as a precious, enormously valuable, and limited resource that needs to be consciously invested for the greatest possible return so that your wealth and success grow.

> *'There's three things that people need to know about business. The first is – time.'*
>
> **Tim Dwyer**, Managing Director of Shirlaws Australia; Partner of BoB (Business of Brand) Group; creator of the Growth Metrics Program

You need to consciously shift your focus – business owners who take the time to learn the skill of *time investment* will gain an enormous advantage over those who continue to think about time as something that just needs to be *managed*.

☑ Write down three ways you could use this strategy:

1. _____
2. _____
3. _____

☐ This strategy is a priority for me.
☐ I have implemented this strategy.

Choice

No business journey is mapped in a straight line from day one to fabulous success at day X. Your business journey will include bumps, potholes, road works, traffic jams, detours, flat tyres, accidents, lost or broken parts, setbacks and crashes. You can't control many of these variables. However, you can control how to respond to them – always take the time to think through your options and choose how you will respond.

☑ Write down three ways you could use this strategy:

1. _____
2. _____
3. _____

☐ This strategy is a priority for me.
☐ I have implemented this strategy.

Productivity Versus Efficiency

Embrace a productivity rather than an efficiency mindset.

Efficiency means producing the same outcomes with less resources. *Productivity*, on the other hand, means producing more with the same resources.

With a focus on productivity, when you have the right people in the right roles investing their time on the right tasks at the right time, you can produce more, and better, products and services for your customers with relatively the same amount of work.

So make productivity your focus.

'Remember, what you focus on is what you create.'

Tim Dwyer, Managing Director of Shirlaws Australia; Partner of BoB (Business of Brand) Group; creator of the Growth Metrics Program

'That's what everyone wants – to have more hours and be more productive.'

Maria Hatzistefanis, President/CEO, Rodial Group (Rodial, NIP+FAB)

☑ Write down three ways you could use this strategy:

1. _____
2. _____
3. _____

☐ This strategy is a priority for me.
☐ I have implemented this strategy.

Don't Be Busy

You look busy. You sound busy. You act busy. When you bump into a friend or colleague and they ask you how you are, you respond: *'I'm so busy!'* And they respond: *'Oh! I'm so busy too!'* And then you spend five minutes talking about how busy everyone is.

Have you ever thought about the impression you create with this simple response? It's essentially the same as responding: *'I'm so unproductive!'* Which is a sentence I'm pretty sure has never come out of your mouth.

You need to lose *being busy*. Find a new response: *I'm terrific; I'm happy; I'm moving at pace; I'm winning; I'm bloody awesome; I'm productive!* A positive response sounds a whole lot better than *I'm busy*, it will lift your mood, and it will leave the right impression.

'People used to have in-trays. They did "actual work" from 9 to 5. Productivity has taken a nose dive because people are just being "busy".'

Alexandra Depledge, Founder and CEO, Resi

☑ Write down three ways you could use this strategy:

1. _____
2. _____
3. _____

☐ This strategy is a priority for me.
☐ I have implemented this strategy.

Find A Gap

The best business ideas are those that fill a gap in the market and solve a problem, often a problem you had yourself and which you resolved. If you had the problem, does that mean others – potentially a mass niche – also have the same problem which you can solve?

> 'At University in South Africa, I loved running. And I just started organising and running the events I wanted to participate in. It was an intense incubator and it started everything.'
>
> **Chris Robb**, Founder and CEO, Mass Participation Asia

Take the time to think about whether you are on to a good thing. Get the data and answer these questions:

- Is there a market?
- What is the niche?
- What is their problem?
- How do you solve their problem?
- Who are your competitors?
- Is your offering unique?
- How will you differentiate?

Keep drilling down to ensure that you have identified a market who want and need your solution. Time spent thinking about this is time very well spent.

Michelle Kennedy, Co-Founder and CEO, Peanut

Michelle Kennedy was solving her own problem when she launched Peanut (a friendship app for mums). Her problem was the enormous sense of disconnectedness she experienced moving from the corporate world into motherhood.

Peanut was launched in February 2018 and uses an algorithm, similar to a dating app algorithm, to match up and connect mums by combining their location, interests, the age of their children and other criteria. Peanut is used by over 350,000 mums worldwide, and this membership is growing exponentially.

Like many new mums, Michelle experienced loneliness and a sense of isolation when she had her son:

When so much of your identity is tied up with who you are at work it becomes so confusing to lose that part. And that's true whether your identity is tied to your hobby or your identity is tied to your circle of friends, the same is true – motherhood changes that because you're no longer able to participate in the same way that you were.

I was relieved to take a step out and take a breather from the corporate world but that really lasted half an hour. And then I really wanted to go back and be around people.

There are so many confusing messages and also you feel very guilty. I felt completely unable to say to anyone: 'I miss work a little bit,' or, 'I'm lonely,' or, 'I'm isolated,' or, 'Motherhood isn't exactly how I saw in the Pampers advert.'

Coming from an established and successful tech business (Bumble, the online dating app), Michelle was used to operating in a tech-savvy environment. However, what surprised her when she had her baby was the lack of tech services connecting mums:

Up until this point, every part of my life was using technology and was cool and slick, and whether that was right down to the basics of ordering stuff on Amazon at 2:00 am that I felt like I must need while Finn was feeding, or Instagram, or Uber, or whatever it might be: all of those elements were very cool, very slick, and very technology first.

I was working in the dating industry, and then motherhood comes along and you're like: 'Okay, where's my experience that is tech first here?' It just felt very fragmented and, quite frankly, old school. And it was at that moment when I felt: 'Wow, the expectation of motherhood is that I must have aged or become less cool or become like my mum who doesn't know how to send a text message.'

The feelings of isolation and the frustration of not having readily available information were quickly exacerbated when Michelle's son Finn became sick:

At four months Finn got bronchiolitis and it was really scary. He ended up in hospital and he was there for a week, and it was the worst time ever. I didn't know what bronchiolitis was. I didn't know whether it was something I had done that had caused this. I didn't know how to get any information. I now know, obviously, with the benefit of speaking to people, making a network, making connections, that it's very common among babies. But at that time I couldn't find the detail that I needed and I couldn't find the support, and that was really scary.

Michelle realised she had found a gap in the market, and Peanut filled that gap:

It was really about amalgamating everything that was out there and really fragmented and bringing it into one platform so that your mindset was: Peanut is where I can make connections; where I can seek advice and support; and where I can speak to likeminded women whatever your kind of sway or your likeminded element is – whether you are working for money, whether you're a stay-at-home mum. Whatever it is, you will find women who are like you and likeminded, and I think that was important for me.

'Classlist.com started off as just solving a problem and now it has become a business.'

Susan Burton, Founder and CEO, Classlist.com

'I've run some of the biggest technology functions in big banks and I knew very well that it is very, very difficult delivering what customers now wanted from traditional banking structures.

'I spent a year in FinTech and got to know all these exciting things that businesses were doing, and I took some of those skills into a bank that had been bailed out during the crisis, the Allied Irish Banks, and helped return the bank to profitability.

'Technology had changed, people were shopping differently with Amazon, they were buying their music differently from iTunes. Everything had changed – but banking hadn't changed.

'I knew there was so much more that could be done in the banking industry. I knew there was an opportunity to bring that new technology, that new experience to customers for the first time.

'I founded and run a business which is doing things that have never been done before. It's a technology business, it's a bank, and it has great people who help me create something together. And I'm terribly fortunate to have all of that.'

Anne Boden, Founder and CEO, Starling Bank

'I saw a bit of a gap between what the big PR agencies were doing well (massive scope but poor match-making between clients and journalists) and what freelance PR agencies did well (match-making between clients and journalists, but with no scope). And I thought there must be a middle ground where I can set up a niche agency which does the best match-making and has huge scope. As a really targeted niche we are very attractive to small to medium enterprises in facility management, architectural design and real estate, who want a PR firm they can partner with.'

Cathy Hayward, Founder and CEO, Magenta

☑ Write down three ways you could use this strategy:

1. _____
2. _____
3. _____

☐ This strategy is a priority for me.
☐ I have implemented this strategy.

Be Courageous

You know those businesses you read about with a brilliant service or a brilliant product and you think: how is it that no-one else thought of that?

But that's the thing – there are probably plenty of people who have had the same or a similar idea, but they just didn't take the leap. In part, because of the hard work involved; in part, because of the enormous time commitment and determination required; in part, because of the financial risk involved in leaving what they currently do (and earn good, regular money from) for the unknown; and in part because of the fear of failing.

But that's what being in business is all about.

Business owners and entrepreneurs are extraordinary that way – you are risk takers. Plus, if you have a great idea and you don't take the leap, someone else will. Damn them.

Stop **wasting your time (1)** thinking about it – be courageous.

> *'I grew up during the Zimbabwean independence war. At 15 I slept with a gun next to my bed. I had friends who died in the war. That gave me incredible perspective about courage and about life. Take a chance. Have courage.'*
>
> **Chris Robb**, Founder and CEO, Mass Participation Asia

Andrea Loubier, Co-Founder and CEO, Mailbird

Andrea Loubier has been recognised as one of the top female entrepreneurs in South East Asia. She is Co-Founder of Mailbird, an email management software system designed to better match client workflow management across multiple devices, channels and apps. Mailbird has been nominated by PC World as one of the best productivity tools for the business person, IT World named Mailbird the best email client for Windows, and Microsoft nominated Mailbird as Startup of the Day:

The idea came about by just talking to people about their frustrations with email. So many people were stuck swimming upstream against email.

I started talking about this online to some other entrepreneurs who were working out of Bali. It felt right. So, I quit my job in Ohio, took a leap and came to Bali to build an email company.

My main advice is to not focus on the problems – don't think, well I can't start a company because I don't have these skills. Instead, look at what you do have and roll with that. Think about what you want to do and what will make you happy and what sort of life you want to live and go for it. It does take a bit of bravery. But if you want it bad enough you will find a way to get there.

☑ Write down three ways you could use this strategy:

1. _____
2. _____
3. _____

☐ This strategy is a priority for me.
☐ I have implemented this strategy.

What Type Of Business Are You Running?

Your time commitment to your business, along with where you need to focus your effort, will vary vastly depending on whether your business is a lifestyle business or a scalable business.

A lifestyle business is one that generates sufficient income to provide a desired lifestyle and includes time for interests outside the business. A scalable business, on the other hand, is designed to grow very big as quickly as possible to provide a return to investors.

Are you running a lifestyle business or a scalable business?

This is a decision you need to make early in your business journey so that (apart from questions of investment, equity sharing, staff, skills, advisers and so on) you can design the right business model; develop the right business plan; and understand the time commitment you need to make to your business.

> *'Time is our most precious resource. Simply put, it's finite. And for entrepreneurs in particular, time is "the" scarcest resource, especially when the business is in its early stages. Founders wear many hats and are juggling corporate admin with customer services, product development and office management. When you take external investment the balance changes: it's important to bring in people who can free up your time to do your highest value work.'*
>
> **Sarah Wood**, Co-Founder and Chair, Unruly

> *'What we realised out of the whole experience [of our first business] was that some businesses should grow organically and some are back-able by heavy finance. With some businesses, it's*

difficult to scale quickly and maintain the integrity and the quality of the service. That was one of the big mistakes we made. It was a huge learning.'

Alexandra Depledge, Founder and CEO, Resi

'We haven't focused on growth, we have focused on engagement. Once you nail engagement, go for scale.'

Susan Burton, Founder and CEO, Classlist.com

Of course you can pivot at any time and ultimately scale a lifestyle business or put a management team into your scaled business and wind back your direct involvement – but focus your attention and time on one strategy at a time.

☑ Write down three ways you could use this strategy:

1. _____
2. _____
3. _____

☐ This strategy is a priority for me.
☐ I have implemented this strategy.

Think Like An Athlete

As a business owner and entrepreneur, you are an athlete. You need stamina; you need to know when to go hard and when to go slow; you need a game plan; you need to pace yourself; and you need to know when to play defence and when to play offence.

Joy Foster, Founder and Managing Director, TechPixies

From 2004 to 2007, Joy Foster was a member of the US Archery team. She also rowed at an elite level, competes in ironman competitions and marathons, and is married to an Olympic Gold Medallist. She is an athlete.

Her business, TechPixies, up-skills women who have been out of the workforce for an extended period on how to use technology to help them return to work, change careers, or start their own business. The TechPixies program provides a combination of hard skills (mostly technology based) and soft skills (for example, communication and time management).

Having played hard and with success as an athlete and in business, Joy is well placed to compare the entrepreneur mindset to the mindset of an athlete:

I think athletes know that to win, they must take risks. I quit my job to train full time for the Olympics – even if I didn't make it, I quit everything to do it. And that's a trait of an entrepreneur – a risk taker. Also not wanting to do the 'normal' thing – when everyone else was going out and getting a job I was going and shooting arrows every day.

'There are lots of parallels between the world of business and professional athletes – a lot of skills roll over. To execute to your absolute potential in both disciplines requires guts, grit, determination, focus and resilience. Both disciplines also require you to rid yourself of the excuses that stop you from reaching your full potential.'

Brant Garvey, Paralympian and Motivational Speaker

> ☑ Write down three ways you could use this strategy:
>
> 1. _____
> 2. _____
> 3. _____
>
> ☐ This strategy is a priority for me.
> ☐ I have implemented this strategy.

Business With Passion

You need to love your business because it will consume a lot of your time.

This is what is so wonderful about running your own business (that, and not working for 'the man') – you get to live and breathe your passion every single day. As the saying goes – do what you love and you will never work a day in your life.

'It's about genuine people trying to solve genuine problems. Money is not the end game. Once you have a story behind your business and a passion, your company just comes to life.'
Devika Wood, Founder and CEO, Vida

Anne Boden, CEO and Founder, Starling Bank

A career banker, Anne Boden has an enormous passion for her industry and for helping her customers.

In 2012, Anne became Chief Operating Officer for Allied Irish Banks and was responsible for helping tens of thousands of Irish citizens who had suffered significantly in the Global Financial Crisis. However, this stint was also frustrating for Anne – she was becoming increasingly dissatisfied with traditional banking, and she saw a massive gap in the market. Technology meant that people were buying differently and were having different experiences, and banking simply wasn't keeping up.

In 2014 Anne founded the fully online Starling Bank in England. It isn't every day you meet someone who owns a bank. Anne explains how it happened:

Well, after 30 years in traditional banking in lots of front-office and back-office roles in the financial services industry, I decided that banking was broken and we could do with a new bank. So I quit my job to start a bank.

As you do.

Her enthusiasm for her business is infectious: 'Isn't it exciting!?', she asks when we meet in London in her open-plan office.

Hell yes, it is.

Anne explains her passion:

I think what I love about it is the fact that, well there's so much adrenaline.

Generally I'd say to people that you have one life and one career, so do things you enjoy. I'm pretty horrified that people stay in jobs that they're not enjoying and feel obliged to do things that they find painful, because all jobs are different and we all resonate with something.

I set out to get a full banking licence and I didn't want to use anybody else's technology. I wanted to build the technology from scratch. I wanted to have direct access into all the payment schemes.

I sat down to do something which was pretty tough – nobody builds banks.

Stop compromising and find and live your passion. Anything less is just a **waste of your time (1)**.

> *'My main time management tip for anybody who is setting up their own business is love what you do because you will be sacrificing other interests. So you really want to make sure that the business you're in is something that you would want to be spending your Sunday afternoons reading about and researching about anyway. Because then it's not a chore and it's not a sacrifice – it's just an incredible opportunity to take control of your own destiny and build something with a lasting impact and legacy.'*
>
> **Sarah Wood**, Co-Founder and CEO, Unruly

> *'It is better to do something that you love because whether it is hard or not, it just becomes relative at that point.'*
>
> **Anu Acharya**, CEO, MapMyGenome

☑ Write down three ways you could use this strategy:

1. _____
2. _____
3. _____

☐ This strategy is a priority for me.
☐ I have implemented this strategy.

Business With Purpose

Research consistently shows that businesses with a deep-seated purpose for making the world better consistently outperform businesses that do not have such a purpose. And, as the owner of your business, that purpose really comes down to you.

'The purpose of business is to create the maximum value exchange in the least amount of time, while having the most amount of fun.'

Tim Dwyer, Managing Director of Shirlaws Australia; Partner of BoB (Business of Brand) Group; creator of the Growth Metrics Program

'Our vision has always been to be the team and the tech that transforms advertising for the better.'

Sarah Wood, Co-Founder and CEO, Unruly

Devika Wood, Founder and CEO, Vida

Devika Wood grew up helping to care for her grandmother who suffered from dementia, schizophrenia, epilepsy and Alzheimer's.

Over 12 years, Devika saw 150 different carers come through her home and knew there had to be a better way for families to source home-based care. She founded Vida when she was 26, and invested in it a mission to promote health and wellness in the home, and to help families who are caring for a sick or elderly family member at home:

I was a carer for my grandma for 12 years, from the age of 10 until the age of 22, and it was the most harrowing experience. We asked for

help from social services and they could only allocate us 15 minutes in the morning and 15 minutes in the evening. I was thrown into this caring role. The lack of consistent care support – we had 150 carers turn up – just made her so much worse and it caused so much friction in our family.

On top of that, my mum and dad worked and had no way of knowing whether a carer had turned up, what they had done when they turned up, or whether they had even come into the house. And while my grandma spoke English, when she got dementia she reverted back to Hindi and no-one spoke her language. So there were communication barriers on top of the confusion, and that's no way to live. You deserve to live with dignity.

And I just watched her…kind of…it was almost like a puppet in a television show, but it wasn't funny. It was just terrible.

So, with Vida, what we are trying to do is change that. We use technology to empower family and next of kin to stay in touch with the carers and to monitor the care at home to get real-time data into our office to help us provide more focused care. The other side is making sure carers are incentivised and that there is career progression for them. We want to retain carers in the industry, so we do a lot of up-skilling.

Plus we match carers with the right client – we have developed a matching algorithm with hard and soft requirements; for example, we need a carer with dementia experience who speaks Spanish, and it will spit out the top five carers within a 30-minute radius.

The focus is to provide person-centred care with a maximum of four carers – that is my purpose because of what my grandmother went through. Four is good compared to 150!

Your purpose is not just to make money. Money is not a purpose – it's just an enabler that gives your business legitimacy. There needs to be more. And if you get your purpose right, this will contribute to your bottom line anyway.

So what is *your* purpose? Take the time to get this right.

'There is a mission behind Peanut and what we do – it is to create something that really symbolises and encapsulates modern motherhood.

'I always wanted to have a product which represented modern motherhood, and that means in every single guise. That means in respect of your relationship with your partner or your family or your friends or your work, money, or any of those things.

'And therefore even on the worst days, to know that there are women who are using this product who will have a different experience of motherhood because of it – it's a no-brainer. However bad my day is – that it means that the start of their day or their journey might be completely different because of Peanut, it's a really wonderful driver for me.

'I feel really proud of Peanut and the team who work tirelessly to make it.'

Michelle Kennedy, Co-Founder and CEO, Peanut

'At TechPixies our purpose is to help women get back into the workplace – either by working for someone else, becoming a freelancer and working for themselves, or starting a business and employing others. Women are 50% of the population, they should be 50% of the workforce too and not forced out or into lower

skill-set jobs just because of a career break. We want them in well-paid positions, and effecting change at the highest levels.'

Joy Foster, Founder and Managing Director, TechPixies

'Originally it was just about doing what I previously thought was impossible for me. But sharing that journey has enabled other people to do what they thought was impossible for them – and that has become the overarching purpose – inspiring people beyond their excuses to do things they previously thought they couldn't do.'

Brant Garvey, Paralympian and Motivational Speaker

Leverage All Of Your Skills

You are the sum of all your parts.

Regardless of what business you are in, identify all of the multitude of skills you have and bring them into the business with you. This is what will make your business truly unique.

Sarah Wood, Co-Founder and Chair, Unruly

Unruly, which was acquired by News Corp in 2015 for $176 million, is a marketing technology company that uses emotional audience data and user-friendly video formats across premium websites to massively increase viewer engagement, brand performance and publisher revenues.

Sarah Wood has been named as Entrepreneur of the Year by City AM, one of 15 Women to Watch in Tech by Inc., one of the Forbes 10 London-Based Entrepreneurs to Watch, and one of CNBC's UK tech industry's top women entrepreneurs.

I met Sarah at the Unruly head office in London in the games room – which is jam packed with every possible game you ever played growing up. Sarah actually caught me in a tryst with 'Simon' (the electronic memory game, circa 1976). Needless to say both the Unruly office space and Sarah are insanely cool.

Having built an uber cool marketing technology company, naturally I started off asking Sarah if she started Unruly off the back of a strong technology background:

No, on the contrary, I have a background in humanities – 18th-century American literature to be precise!

However, it's quite common for entrepreneurs to move across seemingly disparate disciplines and industries as we enjoy exploring new ideas and making connections between different fields.

For me, digital has always been about culture, communication and the democratisation of content rather than being about the technology itself. If you have a passion for culture in the 21st century then you need to understand what technology is available and how you can harness that technology to communicate ideas effectively, at speed and scale. Digital technology is a game changer for all sectors – whether you're in financial services, content creation, health or education.

'Archery was really, really good for my mental training. Later, as an entrepreneur, when my kids were little and I was working on stuff, they would be talking to me and I wouldn't actually hear them and my daughter and my son would say: "Mummy, I'm talking to you!" And actually that was a trait I took away from archery. The ability to have laser focus on something.

'Rowing taught me how to be part of a team. It's about getting along with people and realising that everyone contributes to the win, not just you.

'My most recent sport, triathlon, is more about stretching myself personally, trying to go further and faster, beat my previous times and challenge myself to reach a new level.

'There are really good pieces from each of my three sports that I've brought into everything I do now.'

Joy Foster, Founder and Managing Director, TechPixies

'I was a lawyer for a number of years, trained as a lawyer, and I hated being a lawyer but I think what it does – a legal grounding – is it gives you an understanding of how to think and how to be succinct and how to cut to the chase and how to research and how to dig.

'It's amazing, the life skills you get out of being a lawyer. I'm always saying that my sole, single skill that leads to my success is that I can read huge amounts of turgid information and pull out the relevant part. Because that's kind of what we're trained to do – and I take that enormous analytical thing and apply it to my natural creativity.'

Geeta Sidhu-Robb, CEO, Nosh Detox

☑ Write down three ways you could use this strategy:

1. _____

2. _____

3. _____

☐ This strategy is a priority for me.
☐ I have implemented this strategy.

Hustle Until You Can Almost Afford Not To

In the early stages of your business it's critical that you are involved in every aspect of the business so that you can be confident you are doing exactly what you have promised the market you will do.

You need to be integrally involved in:

- business planning
- product and service development
- marketing
- sales
- positioning
- social media
- PR
- pricing
- invoicing
- the customer experience

- your pitch
- who you will partner with
- data collection and analysis
- framework and process development.

And so on.

You need to be across every single thing, at least initially, so that you know your business has exactly the right foundations in place.

And then build your team.

Chris Robb, Founder and CEO, Mass Participation Asia

When I was 25 I emigrated to Australia from South Africa. I had $15,000 in my pocket. I was following my passion to create mass participation sporting events, and I just said to myself: 'I'm going to make this work.' I had delivered the concept of mass participation sport in South Africa at university and I knew that the same concept was not being delivered in Australia. I had a week of sleepless nights before I left, but in the end I reasoned: 'What is the worst thing that could happen?' – I might fail, but then I could just go back home.

I probably hustled for too long. In fact, I still hustle. But the hustle is always going to be there when you are an entrepreneur. I love the hustle. For me, the hustle isn't about creating material opportunities. The hustle is about generating incredible 'money can't buy experiences' – like when I was in the lead car in front of the Marathon at the 2000 Sydney Olympic Games. The richest man in the world could not have bought that experience. That's what makes the hustle such a pleasure. I have people stop me in the street and tell me that I have changed their lives by introducing them to cycling or running. That's what the hustle is about. It's not about making millions, it's about making a difference.

Hustle also creates opportunity. A big part of hustle for me was and always has been the hustle to find and create the ultimate partnerships. When I started my first business at 25 the hustle helped me attract Deloitte as a partner. That partnership allowed me to quickly expand across Australia. Similarly, creating and building the right partnerships gave me the opportunity to take my business to Asia – something I never thought I would do.

There are days when you are tired and you question what you are doing, but in the end if you are running a business that you love, and you are working with Purpose and Passion, then the hustle isn't really work.

'You have to hustle. Nothing is given to you and I think that entrepreneurs who say: "Oh this happened to me...", I just do not know anyone who succeeded without hustle.'

Maria Hatzistefanis, President/CEO, Rodial Group (Rodial, NIP+FAB)

'I knocked on a lot of doors. Quite a few people helped me – but basically I funded the business myself for two years until two years in I raised £48 million.'

Anne Boden, CEO and Founder, Starling Bank

'In the early days no task is below you. I have worked with lots of clever people who weren't prepared to undertake the less intellectually inspiring tasks. They failed.'

Susan Burton, Founder and CEO, Classlist.com

'When you are CEO of a start-up, you are really Chief Everything Officer.'

Sunita Maheshwari, Chief Dreamer and Loop Closer, Teleradiology Solutions

---

☑ Write down three ways you could use this strategy:

1. _____
2. _____
3. _____

☐ This strategy is a priority for me.
☐ I have implemented this strategy.

You Must Have Grit

Thank goodness you love what you do, because being an entrepreneur and owning and running a business or suite of businesses is really, really hard work.

There's no such thing as 'overnight success'. There's no such thing as 'just being lucky' or 'just being in the right place at the right time'. There's no such thing as 'great rewards for little effort'. Any stories you hear along these lines are just fairy tales.

While there may be an element of luck or good timing – this alone is not enough. If you want your business to succeed you need to work your arse off; you will get knocked down, but you need to keep getting up; you will fail; you will have sleepless nights; you will have bad months; you will need to pay others (suppliers, consultants, staff) before you pay yourself; and you will often feel very lonely or unsure or inadequate or scared or tired or frustrated.

If you want easy, get a job.

'It's funny, on Instagram the other day – I have the Instagram account which shows all the more interesting and glamorous parts of my life – but really I am generally here all day in the office. But I had a picture on Instagram with a celebrity and someone responded: "I want your job! I want your life!" But that is not my job.

'I do find there are a lot of people who see a couple of cool moments and they think this is all you do. And that's a misconception. But I guess it wouldn't make interesting Instagram to post meetings or checking stock at the warehouse all day.

'A lot of people do not understand the work that it takes to grow a business. It's a lot of work.

'I would have told my 18-year-old self that things will be okay at the end. When I started the business I would have sleepless nights almost every night, worrying about the next day and asking, "Will my business survive another day?" If you persevere things will work out in the end. But I didn't know it at the time. I think now I'm a lot calmer.

'You do face challenges every single day regardless at what level the business is, so having a long-term view and not worrying about

the daily problems that you face at the beginning and having the vision for the long term is important.'

Maria Hatzistefanis, President/CEO, Rodial Group (Rodial, NIP+FAB)

'I think if you knew how hard giving birth was going to be you wouldn't do it in the first place. But then, oh how glorious that child is when they arrive. Being in business is the same.'

Joy Foster, Founder and Managing Director, TechPixies

'You look at good entrepreneurs and there is a certain amount of hard work and talent and grit and then there's a certain amount of just timing and luck.'

Alexandra Depledge, Founder and CEO, Resi

Cathy Hayward, Founder and CEO, Magenta

Cathy was working as a journalist in the niche of facility management when she identified a gap between what big PR agencies and small freelance PR professionals were offering their clients. Magenta has been operating for seven years and has expanded from the UK across Europe, and beyond facility management into architectural design and real estate. Cathy travels extensively for work:

There's a lot of drinking bad coffee in naff places around the world – it's not the glamorous idea of travel, where your children think you're sitting in first class sipping champagne. The reality is really different, and most of the time you're kind of glued to your laptop or you're in client meetings. Like yesterday, I was in Brussels in the cab and I was chatting to the client and I suddenly thought: I never just look out the window and see the city that I'm in. I've been to conferences in some amazing places and haven't really seen very much of them.

'I didn't realise how tough it would be.

'Every day is a day that you have to fight for your business. Every day you have to make sure your business is performing well, that you're fighting to look after your customers, and that you react. Customers say great things and they say horrible things and sometimes they say them both together. You must take both on board and do something about it and improve the organisation's act all the time. That's quite bruising if you're an entrepreneur, if it's your business.

'It's so, so important that everything that goes right and everything that goes wrong gives you the energy for the next stage.'

Anne Boden, CEO and Founder, Starling Bank

'I paid my team before I paid myself, and actually when things got really tight for my family because I hadn't been taking a salary, I then had to restructure the whole business and let a bunch of people go. This was for two reasons: (i) to keep the business going; and (ii) to take care of myself. It was hard.'

Joy Foster, Founder and Managing Director, TechPixies

'It's those with grit who are the ones who make it. Having grit goes hand in hand with having the right support team – the people who help pick you up to make sure you keep going when it gets tough.'

Chris Robb, Founder and CEO, Mass Participation Asia

'Even bad days count.'

Brant Garvey, Paralympian and Motivational Speaker

☑ Write down three ways you could use this strategy:

1. _____

2. _____

3. _____

☐ This strategy is a priority for me.
☐ I have implemented this strategy.

Set Audacious Goals

Take the time to set some genuinely audacious goals for your business. **Don't waste your time (1)** shooting for vanilla.

Set ambitious annual, monthly and daily goals.

The act of goal setting will give you clarity over your long-term vision for the business while providing you with a powerful injection of short-term motivation. Having goals will also help you:

• prioritise your **key tasks (94)**

• stay **single focused (120)**

• **reject (52)** what's **wasting your time (1)**

• **say no (25)** to what's not the absolute **best use of your time (20)** .

The act of considering, writing down, and then sharing weekly progress against your goals with your **posse (81)** means you are much more likely to achieve your goals.

Set goals that are clearly aligned to your **business purpose (11)**.

Write down your goals using clear and precise language expressed in the present tense.

Start with your big-picture life goals – where do you want to be in 10 years with respect to: business; finances; family and lifestyle; personal development; health; community engagement; spirituality, and so on.

Use **mind mapping (89)** to break down each big, audacious goal into smaller, bite-sized, task-oriented goals – what can you do today, this month, in the next six months, or in two years that will get you closer to your 10-year plan?

These bite-sized goals then feed into your **business plan (16)**; your daily **to-do list (92)**; and the tasks you consciously choose to give airtime to and those which you consciously choose to **reject (52)**.

And don't lose sight of the fact that we rarely follow a straight line towards achieving our goals – in fact, the tangents, turns and opportunities that arise simply by virtue of the goals we set out to achieve can often be more important, impactful and satisfying than the goals we originally set.

Glen Carlson, Co-Founder, Dent Global

Glen Carlson co-founded Dent Global in 2010 and has grown it into an international world-leading business accelerator for small, entrepreneurial, service-based businesses. Dent has worked with thousands of business owners internationally via the 'Key Person of

Influence Accelerator', with a focus on helping them become more visible, valuable and scalable:

Audacious takes more time than people think.

We talk a lot about doubling speed – for example, McDonald's have doubled their value 15 times – so when you crunch the numbers, the doubling speed for McDonald's (from one store, to two, then double that, then double that…) is about every 4.2 years; and Nike's doubling speed is about every 3.2 years. Dent is currently doubling every 2.7 years (over the last seven years). So if we keep trucking for another 50 years, that gives us an iconic global brand.

That's our big audacious goal. To have Dent as the go-to brand for entrepreneurs and small businesses valued at under $20 million.

'I'm like: "Here are our goals" and everybody in my office is like: "Can you set more realistic ones?" And I'm like: "No, I don't do realism, it really is overrated."

'So that is, I think, the core: realism is what you make it. Where I am not growing as a business is where I am not growing as a person, and I believe that 100%.'

Geeta Sidhu-Robb, CEO and Founder, Nosh Detox

'In the beginning I started with very humble, simple goals. One was to lose weight and control that. Another was to be able to run 100 metres. I set really simple, easy goals, and being able to achieve those gave me a lot of confidence and momentum to go bigger and crazier.

'And now I'm always setting goals in all aspects of my life: be that my personal life, my sporting life or my business life. Those goals get evaluated all of the time – I'd say daily, weekly – and I'm always looking for ways that I can improve on what I'm doing and therefore the goals get adjusted.'

Brant Garvey, Paralympian and Motivational Speaker

'I have a whiteboard next to my desk. My BIG goals are listed. I have a smaller "to-do" list which I email to myself with updates (usually daily), deleting what's been achieved and adding what needs to be done. This works for me. I'm a visual person so I like to see things in pictures and in print, which helps me focus on bigger picture stuff. It's like: "In five years I want to be doing XYZ in life"; so it pushes me to consider, how does what I'm doing now with my business impact the outcome I desire? Lifestyle comes first; my business moulds itself around what I want to achieve in my life.'

Catherine Cervasio, Director, ALUXE Pty Ltd

Write down three ways you could use this strategy:

1. _____
2. _____
3. _____

☐ This strategy is a priority for me.
☐ I have implemented this strategy.

Write A Business Plan

You run a business. You love what you do. You have a fantastic product or service that provides a unique solution for your customers' problems. The challenge is that you are so focused on working *in* the business that you don't have the time to work *on* the business and to strategically plan for the future.

While you know you need to take the time to gain absolute clarity over your next big steps, you are simply too busy. And the very real risk is that you won't make the time to plan. You won't grow. You will miss opportunities. And you will stagnate.

When it comes to business planning, the key challenges business owners face are:

1. You don't have the time for strategic planning – administrative and delivery tasks take all of your time and focus.

2. You own the business but you don't control the agenda – your day is completely reactive.

3. You have so many balls in the air that you worry you won't be able to maintain the pace – and how many balls can you really afford to drop?

Don't waste your time (1) or money starting or running a business without a considered, written business plan.

Preparing a detailed business plan up front takes time, but will ultimately save you a lot of time and angst down the track. You know your starting point, and you have big ideas about where you want the business to be in 1, 2, 5 and 10 years' time, but without the GPS instructions it will take you a lot longer to get there.

You can access business planning information and resources from government or industry led business websites; consult your **posse (81)**; or tap into your **mentors (80)** and advisers.

'We need to be able to move quickly and respond to the market but we also need to take time out to reflect and to have our long-term plans to understand where are we heading.'
Sarah Wood, Co-Founder and CEO, Unruly

'Think long term before making any major decisions. Life flies by, so the earlier you start planning for the long term, the better.'
June Sarpong, MBE

'Last year I did a half-ironman. I followed a 32-week plan and worked with a coach. Throughout the seven hours there were tough parts but I knew in the back of my mind I'd done all the work to get there so I was going to be okay.

'A decade earlier I competed in two marathons without any plan whatsoever. I was fit from rowing and I thought: "Okay, I'm rowing 8 to 10 hours a week so I can do a marathon." But those marathons were really painful, particularly the second one. My brain thought I could do it but I mean, I could barely walk at the end and it was really painful, and I thought: "If I ever do this again I'm going to train for it properly."

'I think business is the same – and it took me a long time to see the value of getting a plan in place for my business. At first I wanted to see what would happen and see where this was going to go, but actually it was advisers and funders that said:

"No, you have to have a plan, you have to map it out because people who have a plan are more likely to succeed."

'Ever since we've had a business plan in place, we've set and beat our targets and grown year on year, every single year.'

Joy Foster, CEO, TechPixies and former US Athlete

☑ Write down three ways you could use this strategy:

1. _____

2. _____

3. _____

☐ This strategy is a priority for me.
☐ I have implemented this strategy.

Undertake Regular Business Styling

Your **business plan (16)** is not a once-off piece of work under-taken when you commence the business, never to be revisited again. With the time you start getting back from employing the strategies in this book, spend some of it to ensure you recalibrate your business plan annually with a half-day session of business styling to ensure you are on track and do not fall behind. Include an examination and recalibration of your:

• goals, values and vision

• ideal customer(s)

• unique value proposition (products, services and intellectual property)

- team capabilities (your team includes everyone who does work for you locally or remotely: employees, consultants and contractors) to meet current and future needs
- key deliverables for the next 12 months
- measures for success.

☑ Write down three ways you could use this strategy:

1. _____
2. _____
3. _____

☐ This strategy is a priority for me.
☐ I have implemented this strategy.

Too Old? Rubbish

Don't let your age stop you. With an ageing population, more older business people will be solving the problems they have, which gives them a product or service that could also be in demand across a big (and ageing) niche market.

Hunter Leonard, Founder and CEO, Silver & Wise

Hunter Leonard started Silver & Wise in 2016, recognising the opportunity to assist older and wiser individuals start and run a successful first business. When it comes to timing, he comments:

Passion is ageless. It doesn't matter how old you are – if you are really passionate about your business idea then age is irrelevant. I have seen

70 year olds absolutely light up when they talk about the business they are launching or have just launched.

Entrepreneurs do get better with age. People who have had 20-plus years' experience in corporate and then for whatever reason have been unable to get another job are becoming highly successful business people. They have life and work experience, they know how to solve problems, and they generate such a great sense of passion and purpose within their business – it's a new start.

'I've been very fortunate at my age (54) becoming an entrepreneur. I think it's more to do with never being satisfied and knowing that there's an opportunity to do something different, to enjoy yourself even more, and nothing too ... well, not too much can go wrong really when you look at the upside rather than the downside.'

Anne Boden, CEO and Founder, Starling Bank

☑ Write down three ways you could use this strategy:

1. _____
2. _____
3. _____

☐ This strategy is a priority for me.
☐ I have implemented this strategy.

(Hourly) Rate Yourself

Your time is money.

I'm not talking about the income you pay yourself from the business. I'm talking about the actual dollar value you generate for your business. This is what your time is worth.

If you have a business model where you charge your clients an hourly rate then this rate is the value you should put on your time, all of the time. If you have a business model where you charge your clients per product or service, then use the following equation to place a value on your time:

$$\frac{\text{Gross annual sales}}{1880} = \text{Your hourly rate}$$

Your hourly rate, for the purposes of this strategy, assumes a standard working week of 40 hours with four weeks annual leave and one week of public holidays (hence 1880 hours per annum), and excludes business expenses, overheads and taxation.

So, for example:

- if the gross annual business revenue is $200,000, your hourly rate is $106

- if the gross annual business revenue is $500,000, your hourly rate is $266

- if the gross annual business revenue is $800,000, your hourly rate is $425

- if the gross annual business revenue is $2,000,000 your hourly rate is $1064.

This is not an exact figure, however it provides a reasonable approximation of your rate – and in fact, you want your hourly rate to be as high as possible because this will genuinely help you to start valuing your time the way you value your money.

Jason Cunningham, Co-Founder, The Practice, and Media Personality

Jason Cunningham's focus in his business and in his media commitments is to help business owners understand, articulate and then achieve their financial objectives:

When I first started business 21 years ago my charge-out rate was $27.50 per hour. And back then I used to think: 'When I am charging 10 times that amount that's when I know I will have made it in business'. Fast forward 21 years and I now know that charging your clients by the hour is not the answer. You need to charge based on what value the customer gets from your service or product.

However, you still need to value your time. Putting a dollar value on your time effectively gives you an efficiency rating. How efficient am I being with my time?

☑ Write down three ways you could use this strategy:

1. _____
2. _____
3. _____

☐ This strategy is a priority for me.
☐ I have implemented this strategy.

54

'Put a value on your time so that others value your time.'
Glen Carlson, Co-Founder, Dent Global

Is This The *Best* Use Of My Time?

For every task you perform there will be four potential costs you will incur:

- Financial Cost
- Opportunity Cost
- Emotional Cost
- Physical Cost.

One (or more) of these costs will resonate strongly with you, and you can use this as the cost lens to stress test whether the task you are working on is really the best use of your time.

Focus on the cost that impacts you most deeply, and for every task you perform from now on, every time you find yourself distracted, every time you allow an interruption, and every minute you procrastinate or delay commencing a task, ask yourself this question: *Is this really the BEST use of my time?*

If it's not, make a better choice.

'The reality is that being good at what you do is just a ticket to the game. Your real role is to ensure you focus your time on leveraging the value you have created for your customers in the

most powerful ways. Every day ask – what should I focus my time on?'

Glen Carlson, Co-Founder, Dent Global

'I'm spending much less time on business social media – instead, I'm outsourcing and concentrating on the higher level marketing. I'm also choosing my presenting and business events more carefully. I ask myself: "How is this going to add value to my business?" or, "Is this a good use of my time?" I've also become better at delegating in the office, which is critical as I step back from the day-to-day running of the business.'

Catherine Cervasio, Director, ALUXE Pty Ltd

☑ Write down three ways you could use this strategy:

1. _____

2. _____

3. _____

☐ This strategy is a priority for me.
☐ I have implemented this strategy.

Financial Cost

You have already **set an hourly rate (19)** and are now consciously thinking about your time as money. So, for example: if your time is worth $100 an hour and you choose to spend an hour of your time a day, every day, on social media then at your hourly rate that is costing you $36,500 of your time a year.

This is not money that is directly coming out of your pocket. Rather, it's symbolic of what your time is worth.

If Financial Cost resonates with you then for every task you choose to perform, ask yourself this question: *is this really the best use of my time* (20) ? *What is this costing me financially?*

If it is not the best use of your time, make a better choice.

'If my hourly earnings are $100 and someone else can do that job for $50 or $70 or $80 or even $90, I outsource.'
Alexandra Depledge, Founder and CEO, Resi

'All four cost lenses resonate with me, however the overarching one for me is Financial Cost because I am an accountant by trade. That then cascades to Opportunity Cost.'
Jason Cunningham, Co-Founder, The Practice, and Media Personality

---

☑ Write down three ways you could use this strategy:

1. _____
2. _____
3. _____

☐ This strategy is a priority for me.
☐ I have implemented this strategy.

Opportunity Cost

For every task you choose to perform there will always be a tradeoff: other tasks you could have spent your time on instead.

If you choose to spend an hour of your day on administrative tasks, what else could you have done with that time? What revenue-generating tasks have you traded off? It's an hour you could have spent:

- winning a new client
- developing a new product
- mind mapping how to expand into a new niche
- strategising potential new partnerships.

If Opportunity Cost resonates with you then for every task you choose to perform ask yourself this question: *is this really* **the best use of my time** (20) *? What is the tradeoff?*

If it is not the best use of your time, make a better choice.

☑ Write down three ways you could use this strategy:

1. _____
2. _____
3. _____

☐ This strategy is a priority for me.
☐ I have implemented this strategy.

'[The cost lens that resonates with me is] probably Opportunity Cost. So I will think very carefully about how I travel and the direction I travel around London so I can use my time effectively on the journey. I will consider very carefully the conferences

I attend and consider the reach of the people I talk to – are they people I always speak to who know me very well, so it might be very good to get together but probably not efficient for them or me? So I think it's Opportunity Cost – I look at what else I could spend my time doing instead of doing that one thing.'

Anne Boden, CEO and Founder, Starling Bank

Emotional Cost

You will either feel good, bad or neutral about the way you spend your time.

For example, if you choose to spend each weeknight working late, when you are tired and less productive, and you then miss your kids' bedtime, how will you feel?

If Emotional Cost resonates with you then for every task you choose to perform ask yourself this question: *is this really **the best use of my time** (20) ? How am I going to feel about this later and how am I making those around me feel?*

If it is not the best use of your time, make a better choice.

☑ Write down three ways you could use this strategy:

1. _____

2. _____

3. _____

☐ This strategy is a priority for me.
☐ I have implemented this strategy.

SMART TIME INVESTMENT FOR BUSINESS

'Is the money worth it for not seeing my daughter? Nine times out of 10 it's not, and so I won't do it.'

Alexandra Depledge, Founder and CEO, Resi

'When I'm messing around in my inbox or I'm ironing a shirt – it's a waste of my time. And I "feel" that waste. I'm not worried about the money it costs me, I just feel it emotionally – it's a feeling of lameness!'

Glen Carlson, Co-Founder, Dent Global

Physical Cost

Some tasks make for pain: physical or mental. If you choose to unload the deliveries at the warehouse without assistance, is there an associated Physical Cost such as a risk of (or actual) back pain, knee pain, fatigue? How is that going to impact you? Will it take you away from revenue-generating tasks?

'With my first business, there was five years of blood, sweat and tears … and hair apparently. I went to get my hair cut and my hairstylist said: "Joy, do you know you've got a bald spot?" I had lost hair from the stress.'

Joy Foster, Founder and Managing Director, TechPixies

If Physical Cost resonates with you then for every task you choose to perform ask yourself this question: *is this really **the best use of my time** (20) ? Is this making for or going to make for pain later?*

If it is not the best use of your time, make a better choice.

✅ Write down three ways you could use this strategy:

1. _____

2. _____

3. _____

☐ This strategy is a priority for me.
☐ I have implemented this strategy.

Saying No

Every time someone asks you to do something for them there will always be an associated cost (at least at a **financial (21)** and **opportunity (22)** level, and possibly at an **emotional (23)** and/or **physical (24)** level). There will often, of course, also be a gain for you – and that is something you need to assess. If it is a task you want to perform, that's great! It's a simple *Yes.*

> *'I say Yes to everything. Everything. First, I love doing it. But also I don't want to say No to anyone because if someone had said No to me at some point maybe I wouldn't be here.'*
>
> **Devika Wood**, Founder and CEO, Vida

But, what if you don't want to say *Yes?*

It can be hard, almost excruciatingly so, to turn down a request for help because many of us are simply programmed to want to help. So, rather than jumping in with an immediate *Yes* each time a request comes your way, remind yourself of the following truths:

1. Every time I say *Yes* to someone else I am saying *No* to myself.

2. There will always be a **Financial Cost (21)** and an **Opportunity Cost (22)**, and sometimes there will be an **Emotional (23) and/or Physical Cost (24)**, to saying *Yes*.

3. My time is money – if someone stopped me in the street and asked me for $100, I'd say *No*.

When a request comes your way, pause to let your brain catch up with your mouth and ask yourself: *is this something I really want to do?* If it is … good, go for it. If it's not, use the following (not mutually exclusive) strategies to help you say *No*:

1. Tell the truth – a lie is only going to dig you a hole and make you feel guilty later (more Emotional Costs).

2. Don't over-explain your decision. Stop talking – you are digging another hole.

3. You don't even need to use the *No* word – try something like: *'Thanks for thinking of me, however I'm working to a deadline at the moment. If anything changes I will come back to you.'*

Another option is to say *Yes*, but make sure it's on your terms: *'Yes, I'm more than happy to review your sales funnel, however I have a few deadlines I have already committed to. I can sit down with you for an hour next month if that works for you?'*

> *'I had to purge. I started to say No to a lot [of requests]. I used to be a bit more of a people pleaser. Now I gladly say No more than I say Yes.'*
>
> **Alexandra Depledge**, Founder and CEO, Resi

June Sarpong, MBE

June Sarpong is one of the most recognisable faces on British television, a media phenomenon, and the only host of her generation who is equally comfortable interviewing business personalities, politicians, celebrities and members of the public. June hosted the Make Poverty History event in London, presented at the UK leg of Live Earth, and co-hosted Nelson Mandela's 90th birthday celebrations in front of 30,000 people in London's Hyde Park, alongside Will Smith. As one of the youngest people to receive an MBE (Member of the British Empire), she has also worked extensively with HRH Prince Charles for 10 years as an ambassador for his charity the Prince's Trust. As a business woman, June is the Co-Founder of the WIE Network (Women: Inspiration and Enterprise); is a panellist on Sky News's flagship weekly current affairs show, The Pledge; and has recently launched her first book, Diversify. She says:

What don't I make time for anymore? I no longer waste time with negative people – it's just not worth it. As you get older you learn to say No.

☑ Write down three ways you could use this strategy:

1. _____
2. _____
3. _____

☐ This strategy is a priority for me.
☐ I have implemented this strategy.

Set Boundaries For Yourself

Setting boundaries is different to saying *No* to other people. Setting boundaries is about saying *No* to yourself. Establish firm boundaries about how and where you are going to spend your time (**is this the best use of my time? (20)**) and be consistent and disciplined.

Think in terms of work boundaries – if you have decided to focus on Product A for 4 weeks then don't get distracted half way through and start chasing other, shiny objects such as a possible Product B, C, D and E. You have made the decision to focus on Product A, this is the boundary you have established – stick to it.

Think in terms of non-work boundaries – if you have committed to a family holiday free from devices and work interruptions, then this is the boundary you have established – stick to it.

Write down three ways you could use this strategy:

1. _____
2. _____
3. _____

☐ This strategy is a priority for me.
☐ I have implemented this strategy.

Embrace Processes

For each task you repeatedly perform in your business, establish and document a process for how the task is most efficiently performed.

It is important to get these processes out of your head and onto paper right from the start – you may be a one wo/man band right now, but as your business grows and you bring on a team to support you, the last thing you or your team will want is for you to be the one reference point for how key processes flow.

The Five Time Investment Basics for Process Development are:

1. Identify the tasks for your business that are both key and repeatable – for example:
   - customer service
   - relationship management
   - invoicing
   - complaints management
   - priority setting
   - decision making
   - customer support
   - thanking referrers.

   And so on.

2. Document how each key process flows.

3. Keep it simple.

4. Educate your team on each process.

5. Don't set and forget – review your processes regularly, at least every six months or annually when you **business style (17)** and engage with your team to identify any additional efficiencies.

'We picked apart our processes to find all of the inefficiencies, and then we put the processes back together. We worked across the entire group. At every step we looked for inefficiencies – how could we do the same thing but faster? Some of the changes we made were so tiny, you would think: should we even bother?

Like changing our drop-down menus and reducing one click, which is just one second of time saved. But across 60 client cases that's one minute. And if you find 60 of those one-minute enhancements, that's an hour.

'We should have been doing this ongoing assessment from the beginning. But we didn't do it in great detail or with great rigour. Now my tagline is: Old is not Gold. What we did, we did – now we are not doing it that way anymore. Now it's an ongoing process of productivity review.'

Sunita Maheshwari, Chief Dreamer and Loop Closer, Teleradiology Solutions

'We consciously take the time to slow down and reflect in order to go faster for the long term; for example, we take the time to have regular retrospectives and futurespectives across the company – two-hour team discussions at the end/start of a project or quarter where people can reflect on what's happened and spot patterns that can be avoided in the future.

'To some managers, it can feel like a time-consuming process at first, but in the long term these reflective sessions empower teams and stop us from repeating the same mistakes.'

Sarah Wood, Co-Founder and CEO, Unruly

📝 Write down three ways you could use this strategy:

1. _____

2. _____

3. _____

☐ This strategy is a priority for me.
☐ I have implemented this strategy.

Leverage Technology

Technology is a massive **productivity (4)** enabler. The right tools, apps and software can allow business owners to do much, much more, and save you a considerable amount of time and money. Think about the following, for example:

- accounting software
- project management software
- marketing tools
- campaign management tools
- task and workflow management software
- collaborations tools
- cloud storage services
- security software
- email management
- document software.

In the wrong hands, however, technology can also be a massive time drain – just how much time do you spend researching, learning how to use, using and generally playing around with these productivity tools, before moving on to the next shiny object?

Be careful not to **waste your time (1)** – business apps are the second most downloaded type of app, right behind gaming apps. Each day, productivity apps are launched as often as dating apps.

Select your technology tools of choice carefully and with the **best use of your time (20)** in mind. Check in with your **posse (81)**, particularly those who are tech savvy, to find out what they use, what works, what doesn't work, and then get them to teach you how best to use the functionality. Don't install multiple tools that do the same thing; do delete the tools that don't work for you; and continue to test and measure your tools of choice to ensure that they are actually delivering you a productivity gain.

Write down three ways you could use this strategy:

1. _____
2. _____
3. _____

☐ This strategy is a priority for me.
☐ I have implemented this strategy.

The 5 SMART Steps

The process I established to help my clients move to a **time investment (2)** mindset is called the *5 SMART Steps*.

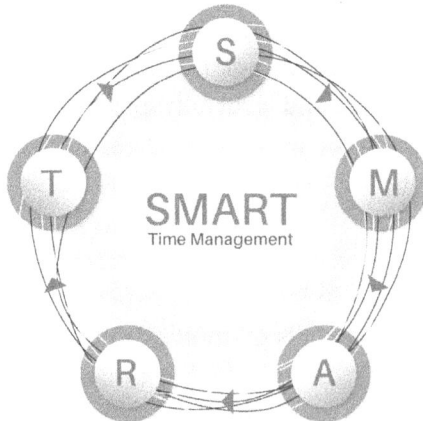

© The 5 SMART Steps, Time Stylers Pty Ltd 2019

- Step 1: **S**elf-aware
- Step 2: **M**ap
- Step 3: **A**nalyse
- Step 4: **R**eframe
- Step 5: **T**ake control

Each of these steps is explained as a strategy below, and you can read more about the *5 SMART Steps* at www.timestylers.com.

> ✍ Write down three ways you could use this strategy:
>
> 1. _____
> 2. _____
> 3. _____
>
> ☐ This strategy is a priority for me.
> ☐ I have implemented this strategy.

Being Self-Aware

It's time to do some self work: what's important to you?

Having absolute clarity over what drives you is central to deciding where you should, and should not, spend your time.

The first step of the *5 SMART Steps* is to be self-aware. Ironically, the reason we rarely take the time to reflect on things like: how do I feel about this life I lead; the time I commit to my business; the people I engage with; the time I devote to my family, friends, community, spiritual and volunteering commitments; and so on – is because we simply don't have the time.

Make the time to think about and identify your:

- **Key time challenges:** what keeps tripping you up, getting in the way and robbing you of time? Where are you **wasting your time (1)** ?

- **Core values:** what values drive your behaviour and what would a values-driven day look like?

Why should you do this? Because you need a baseline against which to reflect on your current time habits and against which to measure the improved behaviours you are about to implement. You also want a very clear understanding of what you are, and are not, prepared to sacrifice your time for.

'In my business I make time for three things: leadership; growth and space.

'Space is key for me. For a long time my day was a series of back-to-back appointments or engagements and people used to say to me – you get so much done each day! But what I eventually realised was that by being back-to-back all day long I was being efficient, but I wasn't being effective.

'That's where making time for space comes in. Having space allows me to take the time to be present, to talk to people, to build relationships, to think about strategy, to focus on leadership and growth, and to connect and engage.'

Jason Cunningham, Co-Founder, The Practice, and Media Personality

'You can't do it all.

'As Unruly grew into a global business I became acutely aware of this, and the importance of mindful prioritisation. There was

time to be with my family, be with the children, make sure that I'm a good mum, and then there was time to grow the business. But there wasn't much left over for anything beyond those two priorities (especially as I always prioritised seven to eight hours sleep a night).

'It wasn't a problem, though, because it was the path I had actively chosen – I love nothing more than the joy that comes with family time and the intellectual challenge that comes from growing a global business!'

Sarah Wood, Co-Founder and Chair, Unruly

'It's really important – something has to give. You cannot have everything.

'So very early on I decided I'm not going to have a social life. It's going to be my family and it's going to be my work. Before I had kids I would go out with my girlfriends and go for lunches and teas, but I just don't have time right now – it has to be family or work and nothing else. It's a tradeoff you make. And I'm okay with that.'

Maria Hatzistefanis, President/CEO, Rodial Group (Rodial, NIP+FAB)

'I didn't make time for friends because I was so busy surviving that I didn't remember that I had to thrive, and that was the biggest time sin I created.

'So last year I was like: "Oh my god, I've literally ignored all my friends and they aren't talking to me, maybe I should go fix this," so I did. And so now I'm super careful to show up. Like yesterday we did the conference all day and in the evening one of my friends was having an event, so I turned up to that even though I wanted to die and go to bed and never leave again.

'That was the biggest thing that I didn't do, make time for friends. And now I do that too, otherwise it won't happen.'

Geeta Sidhu-Robb, CEO, Nosh Detox

'Sometimes you need to flow with things – you need to be a little flexible. A lot of things change in life and don't turn out the way you imagined. Be ready to embrace what comes your way, as long as you keep your core values intact – be kind to yourself if things change.'

Devika Wood, Founder and CEO, Vida

'It impacts your relationships and friendships because people don't really understand how stressful and time consuming it is. Not everyone will stick around you. It's a selfish time.'

Sunita Maheshwari, Chief Dreamer and Loop Closer, Teleradiology Solutions

'Be ready to accept that not everyone will be on this journey with you, and that's okay.'

Michelle Kennedy, Co-Founder and CEO, Peanut

☑ Write down three ways you could use this strategy:

1. _____
2. _____
3. _____

☐ This strategy is a priority for me.
☐ I have implemented this strategy.

Map Your Time

Your business day is made up of a multitude of competing demands on your time. So, how do you know which **time investment (2)** is the best?

To make the right decisions, you need the data.

Where do you spend your time? What habits or rituals do you engage in and when? How often are you **interrupted (124)**? By whom? Do you procrastinate? Are you easily distracted? Is there a pattern to the interruptions and distractions? How often are you on your **device (105)**? How often are you off your device? How many **emails (106)** do you receive? How often are you in your emails? How many **meetings (119)** do you attend? Are they **productive (4)**?

You cannot fully respond to these types of questions about your daily time usage without a full set of data. And without a full set of data you won't be able to make all of the changes you need to make in order to maximise your time spend. Besides, once you see the data you will have a clear idea of exactly how much **time you waste (1)** – which is a great motivator for change.

Step 2 of the *5 SMART Steps* involves mapping three days of your life in detail. It's a personal time audit to clearly identify exactly where you spend your time from the moment you get up to the moment you go to bed: every call; every sale; every customer inquiry; every distraction; every interruption; every transaction; every task or activity for your family; and everything else that makes up the cacophony of your day.

Why? Because you can't know what changes you can make to your **time investment (2)** habits until you know in detail exactly where you spend your time.

To conduct your personal time audit, select two workdays and one weekend day. From the moment you get up until the moment you go to bed, log every task you perform and how long you spend on the task.

Your mapped time will provide you with an incredible amount of valuable data. The more time you map the more poor habits and behaviours you will identify. When you have completed mapping your time you can move on to **analysing your time spend (32)** .

Plus, there is nothing to stop you from mapping your time beyond the three days of data – you will continue to flush out habits and behaviours that you need to change the more days you map.

✏ Write down three ways you could use this strategy:

1. _____
2. _____
3. _____

☐ This strategy is a priority for me.
☐ I have implemented this strategy.

Analyse Your Time

Step 3 of the *5 SMART Steps* gets you to analyse your tasks.

The tasks you perform, as logged in your three days of **mapped time (31)**, will fall into one of four task categories:

1. **Musts:** The tasks that you, and *only* you, can perform.

2. **Wants:** The tasks that you undertake just for yourself – the fun stuff.

3. **Outsource (or delegate if you have a team):** The tasks that someone else can perform for you in return for payment (or for free).

4. **Reject:** The tasks you don't need to do at all, or that you do need to do but which can be done smarter, faster or differently.

It's about getting rid of the low-values tasks (**outsource (39)**) and the no-value tasks (**reject (52)**) to make time for the fun stuff (Wants) and to focus your attention on the tasks that provide the greatest return for your business (Musts), such as a better understanding of your clients and their needs so that you create the space to attract better, higher paying clients.

The outsource and reject categories are where all of the gold of your lost time is buried – this is where you will find and harness hours of time.

Write down three ways you could use this strategy:

1. _____
2. _____
3. _____

☐ This strategy is a priority for me.
☐ I have implemented this strategy.

Reframe

Step 4 of the *5 SMART Steps* is where you take all of the data you have collected and then decide exactly what you are going to **outsource (39)** (or delegate) and **reject (52)** .

☑ Write down three ways you could use this strategy:

1. _____
2. _____
3. _____

☐ This strategy is a priority for me.
☐ I have implemented this strategy.

Take Control

The final step of the *5 SMART Steps* is implementation.

Schedule **deadlines (86)** in your **calendar (96)** for implementing each new **time investment (2)** strategy you have identified in this book.

Repetition and ritual (37) will help you embed and sustain your new time investment behaviours.

☑ Write down three ways you could use this strategy:

1. _____
2. _____
3. _____

☐ This strategy is a priority for me.
☐ I have implemented this strategy.

Conduct An Annual Detox

The *5 SMART Steps* is an iterative process. Like a summer detox program, the idea is to revisit the framework at least annually to recalibrate your personal **time investment (2)** habits.

Over time, some poor habits may slip back in; or you will want to **reject (52)** and **outsource (39)** other tasks because now you know these tasks are not the **best use of your time (20)**; or your circumstances may change, which will require you to reflect on your new business and life **goals (15)** and **values (30)**.

☑ Write down three ways you could use this strategy:

1. _____
2. _____
3. _____

☐ This strategy is a priority for me.
☐ I have implemented this strategy.

Lock In Me Time

Invest time in yourself. Making time for your Wants is crucial to making you a better, happier person, and ultimately a better, happier business owner.

Start from a place of 'me first' in terms of self-care. For every hour you reclaim, lock a Want into your **calendar (96)** and make sure you turn up. That is what you are here for. As business owners, we often put the Wants of others ahead of our own Wants, but in the long run that's not good for you or your business.

'My husband [a former Olympic rower and Gold Medallist] was a rowing coach, and over the years he had lots of young men who went through his programs, and eventually many of them would say: "I have to quit so I can focus on my studies." And he always felt sorry for them because people who study and train actually, ironically, have better time management and actually end up doing both better.

'I was on the US Archery team for four years from 2004 to 2007, and I rowed before that at university and also at high school. And now I'm training for an Ironman, and I think it's true – my business is usually doing better when I'm training. For me training is "me time".'

Joy Foster, Founder and Managing Director, TechPixies

'When it's your passion and your baby you forget about yourself... [But] if you crash, everything crashes.'

Devika Wood, Founder and CEO, Vida

'I have a thing I call "the balance sheet technique" – it all started from the fact that I've been a single parent for so long, and the only person I didn't know how to look after was me.

'And I remember getting super, super ill one day and being on a drip in the hospital and thinking: "Oh my God, if I die my ex will have to look after my kids."

'I just was like: "This is super, super stupid."

'So what I do is I use the balance sheet technique and I think of every day as having a profit and loss account – so on one side I have the things that really matter to me (and that is my exercising, it is drinking water, it is eating healthily, it is yoga, it is meditating and my morning rituals and time with my friends, and time with the kids – whatever). And then what I do is at the beginning of every week I put those priorities into my week, my balance sheet; and then I look at every day and I see the P and L of how I'm winning or losing in that day and I adjust accordingly.

'It makes life very simple because then it's all done. That's what I'm doing, and then everything else is allowed into my schedule around the "profit" items.'

Geeta Sidhu-Robb, CEO, Nosh Detox

'My team all take an hour out on a Monday morning to do a boxercise class together – and we are all so much more productive and engaged as a result. I find it really kick starts my Monday if I've done boxercise – it's such a great feeling, so that hour is well spent.'

Cathy Hayward, Founder and CEO, Magenta

☑ Write down three ways you could use this strategy:

1. _____
2. _____
3. _____

☐ This strategy is a priority for me.
☐ I have implemented this strategy.

Repetition And Ritual

Establishing a new time habit and genuinely locking it in takes work – you need to consciously implement each new strategy with intent. If you do the work, your new time habit will become second nature to you.

Repetition is critical to training your brain to successfully establish and implement new time habits and behaviours. Implement the strategy and then repeat, repeat and repeat again.

Support the act of repetition with a simple ritual. Following a ritual helps establish a new habit: by repeating the ritual each time you implement a new **time investment (2)** strategy, you are reinforcing the better behaviour and helping to train your brain to consciously stay on track.

Try the following simple two-step ritual:

1. Write down on a sticky note the change you are about to make (for example: *Turn off my email alerts*).

2. As you stick the note in a designated place (for example: on the wall next to your computer where you can see it), repeat

the same short mantra each time (for example: *This is NOT the best use of my time!*).

☑ Write down three ways you could use this strategy:

1. _____

2. _____

3. _____

☐ This strategy is a priority for me.
☐ I have implemented this strategy.

Think Outside The Square

Unless you have a load of cashed-up investors or you are yourself super cashed up, in the early days in particular you won't have a bomb to spend on every element of your business. So, take the time to think about where you can save money, what you can do or get for free, and how you can differentiate your business on a budget.

How can you do things smarter?

'I didn't have the money to spend on promoting the products, so I had to find a way to make the product create its own buzz.

'My product Snake Serum contains synake peptide, which is a synthetic ingredient that mimics the effect of viper venom. It was the first product we gave an "outside the box" name to and it got a lot of attention for the brand. People started talking about Snake Serum.

'So we followed this with a product called Dragon's Blood – which contains the sap from a tree – but we are not killing any dragons! No dragons died in the creation of this product!'

Maria Hatzistefanis, President/CEO, Rodial Group (Rodial, NIP+FAB)

☑ Write down three ways you could use this strategy:

1. _____

2. _____

3. _____

☐ This strategy is a priority for me.
☐ I have implemented this strategy.

Outsource As Soon As You Possibly Can

Noting **hustle until you can almost afford not to (13)** , you want to outsource as soon as you possibly can – which is usually before you can really afford it.

'The first three years I did everything for myself. I just focused on the area of the business that most needed me. It would be one day something has gone wrong in production, and one day I need to focus on sales, or one day to meet some journalists and tell my story.

'I quickly worked out what I loved and what I would outsource as soon as I could.

82

'The first person I hired was a part-time accountant. No-one is getting any benefit from me dealing with accounts. And it's not something I love doing.

'The second person I hired, and that was much, much earlier than I could afford them, was a sales manager. I would go to the store and sell my products but I didn't have the experience. I needed someone who could do this.

'I've always invested in good sales people. Always when I've invested a little bit more, it would give the business what it needed to take it to the next level. At the end of the day, sales are everything. Sales will take your business to the next level. It's taking that leap of faith, saying, "These are the skills I need to bring into the business. This is a risk I need to take."

'And at the end of the day what's the worst thing that could happen? You lose three months' salary. But if the person is good they can take your business to the next level.'

Maria Hatzistefanis, President/CEO, Rodial Group (Rodial, NIP+FAB)

The reason you outsource the tasks you don't want to do, don't have the skill set to do well or efficiently, or don't have time to do is to give yourself time for the things you must do or want to do. Go figure.

Based on your analysis of your three days of **mapped time (31)** and the **analysis (32)** of the tasks you performed, highlight each task you have identified as one you can potentially outsource at work.

List these tasks in order of priority based on the following three criteria:

1. What tasks don't I love doing?

2. What tasks will someone else (an expert) be able to perform faster, better and cheaper than me?

3. What tasks when undertaken by an expert will generate the greatest return on time or money for my business?

Having identified target tasks to be outsourced (or delegated if you have a team), set a **deadline (86)** in your **calendar (96)** to progress the identification, engagement and instruction of the best resource to perform these tasks for you.

> *'I don't do a lot of things like cooking or cleaning – they can be done by other professionals. So when you want to cook you do it as more of a hobby. You have to take certain things off your plate so that you can manage.*
>
> *'That also goes to managing a business – if you want to do everything yourself, there is only a certain skill set you have. It is better to have a good team you can delegate to.'*
>
> **Anu Acharya**, CEO, MapMyGenome

☑ Write down three ways you could use this strategy:

1. _____

2. _____

3. _____

☐ This strategy is a priority for me.
☐ I have implemented this strategy.

Focus On Your Strengths And Outsource Your Weaknesses

You can and should only **hustle (13)** for so long. Continuing to wear every hat in your business is simply not sustainable – just how many of you do you actually think there are?

On top of that, are you really, genuinely good at (and/or love doing) all of the many elements that your business needs: from product design and development to production to sales to legal to IT to HR to graphic design to social media to finance to book-keeping to data analytics to coding to web development to writing to translation to…?

And are you really, genuinely good at all of the necessary home-based tasks?

Outsourcing (39) allows you to focus more of your time on the tasks you absolutely love to perform – your **passions (10)** – the very reason you went into business in the first place. If you are a chocolatier, you went into business because you adore making beautiful chocolate. You do not adore, nor are you likely to be very good at, bookwork, payroll, process development or managing a CRM.

'Do the bits you love – set very clear boundaries for your role within the business, and that's around: what do I love doing, what's my passion? They're the bits I'm going to do and I'll find other great people to do the other bits and I'll just leave them alone to get on with it.'

Geeta Sidhu-Robb, CEO, Nosh Detox

'I believe that you should actually do more of the things that you are good at and less of the things that you're not very good at, because it is painful. And lots of organisations get it wrong by encouraging people to be more "well rounded" and they put people into things that they're not very good at in order to build them up and work on their weaknesses.

'We're all much better at doing things that we have a natural affinity for and we're all happier doing it. So don't make an organisation chart so that everybody is equal. Everybody's different.

'Get people to do things they love and it's far less painful for the rest of us.'

Anne Boden, CEO and Founder, Starling Bank

'Whether you call yourself a CEO or Managing Director – if you're the head of the company, and it took me a while to figure this out, that role is very different to any other role.

'In my previous business I couldn't let things go. I'd fly at 30,000 feet where the Chief Executive should be, but then I'd consistently dive down into the detail, and you just can't do that. It wasn't good for the business. It wasn't good for me. It wasn't good for the staff.

'With Resi, I've never been in the detail. That doesn't mean that I don't understand what the customers are saying or what they are experiencing. It just means that I let the team handle the detail and I make the strategic decisions. If you are not involved in the detail it means you are able to take a step back and you are always looking at the big picture.

'Define your role. What are you good at? What are you bad at? What should be one of the first things you should give up? As you continue to grow you need to let things go. Because if you are working all of the hours that god sends, that is a problem. You are the problem.

'Often for a lot of first-time founders, they start doing everything and they continue doing everything and they don't mature. You become the obstacle to growth. Instead, build your team and support them. This is so fundamental for the success of the business as it moves through different phases. It's fundamental to how you invest your time as a leader. How can your company grow?'

Alexandra Depledge, Founder and CEO, Resi

'I call it the Entrepreneur's Bet: can you create more value and wealth by playing to your strengths than it costs to outsource your weaknesses? If you are not willing to make that bet, don't go into business. Or, if you are in business and you are not willing to make that bet, then don't complain that it's a struggle and you have no time.'

Glen Carlson, Co-Founder, Dent Global

Write down three ways you could use this strategy:

1. _____
2. _____
3. _____

☐ This strategy is a priority for me.
☐ I have implemented this strategy.

Business Outsourcing

The best tasks to outsource are those that:

- are low value or not revenue generating; and/or
- you don't enjoy; and/or
- you are not an expert at; and/or
- someone else (an expert in the field) can do a better, faster, or more cost-effective job than you.

By engaging the right people with the right skill sets you not only free up your time for the tasks you excel at and which you love (**Opportunity Cost (22)**), but you also expose your business to the opportunity for growth.

It's time to outsource – any task an expert can do faster, better and cheaper than you is up for grabs.

You are spoilt for choice when it comes to identifying the best person to outsource a task to. Just Google 'best freelance sites [year]' for the top freelance sites at the moment.

'You must never be the bottleneck. That's my goal.'
Geeta Sidhu-Robb, CEO, Nosh Detox

'It got to a stage where we had about 20 schools and I was still the IT person and it was starting to creak, and we had to employ somebody who actually knew what they were doing so we could scale the business. And then we needed some funding. And when

we got an employee and we got some funding, it then grew to the next level and we had a business.'

Susan Burton, Founder and CEO, Classlist.com

'If you can outsource it/delegate it, do so. Don't let yourself get caught up in doing the small things. Gather around you a team you can trust and focus on the big picture.'

Catherine Cervasio, Director, ALUXE Pty Ltd

☑ Write down three ways you could use this strategy:

1. _____

2. _____

3. _____

☐ This strategy is a priority for me.
☐ I have implemented this strategy.

---

50 Jobs You Can Outsource In Your Business

Here is a sample of the types of tasks you can outsource in your business:

1. Email management, email triaging, email templates
2. Calendar management
3. Booking appointments with clients
4. Task organisation
5. Travel arrangements and planning
6. Cloud management

7. Document management
8. Preparing PowerPoint presentations
9. Creating forms
10. Creating document templates
11. Social media management
12. Blog writing and commenting
13. Blog publishing
14. Managing Facebook pages and posts
15. Managing LinkedIn
16. Managing a YouTube account and uploading videos
17. Managing an Instagram account and posting
18. Answering calls
19. Sending invoices
20. Paying bills
21. Personal tasks
22. Website design
23. Website build
24. Website management and maintenance
25. Website analysis
26. Google analytics
27. Google AdWords
28. Payment gateway integration and management
29. SEO writing
30. Link building
31. Keyword research
32. Creating landing pages

33. Press release writing
34. Engaging and managing other consultants (for example, IT, designers, web builders)
35. Sales
36. Bookkeeping
37. Accounting
38. Legal
39. HR
40. IT
41. Data analysis
42. Database building
43. CRM management
44. Campaign design and management
45. Branding
46. Logo design
47. Graphics
48. Podcast creation and publishing
49. Ghost writing
50. Videography

📝 Write down three ways you could use this strategy:

1. _____
2. _____
3. _____

☐ This strategy is a priority for me.
☐ I have implemented this strategy.

Home Outsourcing

Outsourcing is a simple, effective and efficient way to gain back a significant amount of time on the home front.

On the home front, outsourced tasks fall into two categories:

Definition	What to consider
Outsourcing: The tasks you undertake which you are prepared to pay someone else, an expert, to do.	Keep in mind your costs: • **Financial Costs** – if your time is worth $100 an hour and you spend four hours cleaning your home, that is a $400 clean. You can engage a housekeeper for $25–$30 an hour, and because they are an expert they will complete the job in three hours. • **Opportunity Costs** – what else could you do with those four hours? • **Emotional Costs** – how will you feel during and after the clean, having screamed at your family to help you? • **Physical Costs** – will you hurt your back again shifting the furniture to vacuum?
Insourcing: The tasks you undertake for those you live with that they can do for themselves, without pay.	Keep in mind your costs. For example: • if you spend five minutes a day sorting your family's dirty washing, that's 30 hours of your time a year • if you spend 12 minutes a day tidying up all of the 'stuff' your kids leave around the house, that's 73 hours of your time a year. That's nearly two working weeks a year!

Give yourself permission to spend your money to get an expert to help you at home so that you can focus more of your time and effort on what you love. Who wouldn't rather use two hours on a Sunday for a long lunch with friends as opposed to ironing shirts for the week?

Identify everything you currently do around the home that someone else, an expert, can do for you, that you are prepared to pay them for.

The Five Time Investment Basics for Outsourcing at Home:

1. You are not a machine. You cannot do it all, and you do not need to do it all. Stop feeling guilty. Stop thinking: *I should be doing this because it is my house, my garden, my child, my dog.* Give yourself permission to get the help you need at home.

2. Just like outsourcing at work, the simple truth is that there are experts out there who can do certain home-based tasks faster, better and cheaper than you.

3. Make a list of all the tasks you do at home and then rank them in order of what you really, really hate to do. Work through the ranked tasks, decide exactly what you will outsource, and then find the right expert to perform the task for you. If an individual task does not take very long, couple it with other tasks to build it up to at least two to three hours worth of work a week.

4. Thinks about the cost lens that resonates most strongly with you – if you are hesitating, ask yourself: **Is this really the best use (20)** *of my time?*

5. Consciously re-invest the time you reclaim into a Want.

Geeta Sidhu-Robb, CEO, Nosh Detox

Geeta Sidhu-Robb spent over a decade working as a corporate law-yer in London, Moscow and Nairobi, but gave it up when her son was chronically ill with severe allergies and anaphylaxis:

I never wanted to be a lawyer but there we were. So I ran away from that just as quickly as I could.

Her son's illness was actually the inspiration for her business, Nosh Detox – at the time she had three children under seven, had recently divorced, and needed to support her young family while still being available to them:

What I knew to do was to help people get strong and healthy as I had cured my son of eczema and asthma. Then a friend was moaning to me about being fat, so I wrote up a list for her to follow and she lost the extra weight within weeks. She said to me: 'People will pay for this'.

So what we do is we create one-stop holistic health solutions for people who have problems with their wellness. Because there is this very long space of wellness and then you fall off the end and you become ill: and doctors only treat illness. And what we do is we support wellness before you get to that stage.

Despite working in the wellness industry, Geeta learnt the lesson of the need to outsource at home the hard way, after collapsing and being hospitalised for exhaustion:

Since that day when I was in the hospital on a drip I have outsourced. I outsource everything. I mean, I'm Indian and I grew up in Africa so I was used to having help in the house, but I kind of didn't compute that to payment – I didn't want to spend the money. [But now] I have a woman who runs my home and she handles

everything except the bills – she handles the food, the cooking, the
ordering, the washing, the ironing – and I stay out of the way.

'*Up until about 40 years of age, I never had any help for the*
house. I never had anybody helping me with all these various
things. But from about 40 years of age onwards I decided that I
was going to work very, very hard and enjoy everything in my life.

'*I really enjoy work, [and I needed to] eliminate from my life the*
things I didn't love doing.

'*So now I have people who help me get the house organised; and sort*
out my wardrobe and get rid of everything I don't want and take
them to charity shops; and to make sure that if I'm participating in
something I turn up with the right gifts; or whatever.

'*I think up until I was 40 years of age I thought that to have a*
cleaner was selfish or wasn't frugal enough – that it was being
indulgent. It's all about the work ethic.

'*And then I realised that I could do everything I want – I can do*
as much work as possible, because that's what I love. I love work.
And that in some respects [outsourcing] helps others, and [allows
me to] do more of what I like.

'*So many women who can afford these things feel as if they have*
to do it themselves, and [yet by doing it themselves] they are in
turn actually ignoring things that only they can do.

'*I spend a lot of time in the business – this is something I do all*
the time. But that's okay because the things I don't do, somebody
else does for me and I can [either] spend my time doing things for
me or for the business.'

Anne Boden, CEO and Founder, Starling Bank

> ☑ Write down three ways you could use this strategy:
>
> 1. _____
> 2. _____
> 3. _____
>
> ☐ This strategy is a priority for me.
> ☐ I have implemented this strategy.

50 Jobs You Can Outsource At Home

Here is a sample of the types of tasks you can outsource at home:

1. Cleaning
2. Housekeeping
3. Carpet cleaning
4. Window cleaning
5. Meal planning
6. Meal preparation
7. Food shopping
8. Clothes washing, folding and putting away
9. Ironing
10. Nannying
11. Mother's helper (childcare and light household duties)
12. Before and after school care
13. Spring cleaning
14. Decluttering cupboards
15. Decluttering the garage

16. Arranging a hard rubbish collect
17. Sorting unused clothes and toys and dropping at a charity
18. Shopping for and wrapping gifts
19. Gutter cleaning
20. Gardening
21. Mowing
22. Weeding
23. Planting and pruning plants
24. Removing garden waste
25. Dog walking
26. Pet grooming and washing
27. Pet sitting
28. Taking your pet to the vet
29. House sitting
30. Carer or companion for an elderly dependent
31. Home manager or personal assistant
32. Someone to wait for the plumber/electrician/delivery person
33. Someone to assemble flat-packed furniture
34. An expert to program your TV
35. An expert to help with home IT issues
36. Basic home maintenance
37. Packing, unpacking and managing a home move
38. Tutoring
39. Someone to run errands; for example, collecting dry cleaning
40. Someone to pay home bills
41. Someone to collect your mail when you are out of town
42. An expert to style your living space
43. An expert to book your holiday

44. Someone to put out and bring in the bins when you are out of town
45. Someone to sort or itemise your photos
46. Someone to clean your inbox and set up folders
47. Someone to systemise your home office
48. Someone to source and order basics online; for example, undies, socks and school supplies
49. An expert to maintain and clean your car
50. An expert to maintain your pool

> 'Cleaning the toilet has never improved my character, so I'm like: "You know, we're just not going to do that." And my best friend loves to cook and my mother loves to cook and I just don't get it – how can you spend all this time making this stuff and it's gone in 10 minutes? Why would anyone cook? So I pay to have the best food come in and somebody who knows how to make it for me. I outsource all of that stuff because I just don't want to do it. I hate housework too.'
>
> **Geeta Sidhu-Robb**, CEO, Nosh Detox

> 'I would rather outsource things like the gardening and cleaning the house so that I can spend time with my family.'
>
> **Jason Cunningham**, Co-Founder, The Practice, and Media Personality

---

Write down three ways you could use this strategy:

1. _____
2. _____
3. _____

☐ This strategy is a priority for me.
☐ I have implemented this strategy.

Get A Cleaner

Engaging a cleaner is the first task you should **outsource at home (43)**.

Reject (52) any feelings of guilt on this one – yes, it is your home, but that does not mean you are the person who has to clean it. Your time is better spent elsewhere – growing the business or spending quality time with the people you most love.

Can't afford a cleaner just yet? Really?

That inner voice is a voice you need to reject. Regardless of where you are in your business journey, you can afford a house cleaner. If you spend four hours a week cleaning your home, what is that costing you? All four cost layers resonate here, most particularly **Opportunity Cost (22)**. That's four hours you could have spent winning a new client; securing new partnerships; relationship management – all of which contribute to the bottom line of your business.

Make the tradeoff: forego a night out with your mates and pay for a cleaner instead.

✏ Write down three ways you could use this strategy:

1. _____
2. _____
3. _____

☐ This strategy is a priority for me.
☐ I have implemented this strategy.

Don't Clean

And when you have a cleaner – do not clean the house before the cleaner comes. Cleaners have seen worse, trust me.

☑ Write down three ways you could use this strategy:

1. _____
2. _____
3. _____

☐ This strategy is a priority for me.
☐ I have implemented this strategy.

SMART Outsourcing

The number one reason business owners hesitate to **outsource (39)** is that they feel it is a time-consuming process which more often than not does not render the result they want, which means rework (and additional time and cost) for you. And so you think – *it's easier if I just do it myself.*

Wrong – if you continue to do everything yourself you will pretty quickly run out of time. It is not easier for you to do every single task in your business yourself. You just need to learn how to outsource the SMART way.

When you outsource, the aim is for the service provider to deliver the same or a better result than if you undertook the task yourself. Considering this, and the fact that outsourcing will cost you money, the key to getting the best possible result from the service provider the first time is to give clear and specific instructions up front.

The standard (wrong) way to outsource is the SAT method:

SAT outsourcing	Action
Select	Select the best person for the task
Activity	Explain the details of the task
Timeframe	Set a deadline for delivery

For example:

(Select) *Sashi, I want you to* (Activity) *design the social media marketing campaign for our new Product A, anticipating a budget of $X. I want it by next Friday please* (Timeframe).

SAT does not provide the outsource service provider with anywhere near enough information, and it is very unlikely that Sashi will produce a piece of work that you are entirely, or even remotely, happy with.

The better way to outsource is the SMART method:

SMART outsourcing	Action
Select	Select the best person for the task.
Motivate	Explain why the task is important. *This step is often missed when outsourcing. However, it is critical to the success of the task that you explain why the task needs to be done, otherwise the outsource service provider is working on the task without context.*

SMART outsourcing	Action
Activity	Explain the details of the task.
Result	Explain what a good result will look like. *This is another critical step often missed when outsourcing. By explaining what a great result will look like, you are framing the task for the outsource service provider and setting them up for success.*
Timeframe	Set realistic, yet hard deadlines for a mid-point check in, and then for final delivery. Schedule these deadlines in your calendar and put the task out of your mind.

For example:

(Select) *Sashi, our new Product A hits the shops in six months* and (Motivate) *it is absolutely critical that we have enough runway with customers via our social media channels so that they are really excited about what is coming. I want you to* (Activity) *design the social media marketing campaign for our new Product A, anticipating a budget of $X.* (Result) *A great result will be a five-page proposal with a one-page strategy for each of our major social platforms: Facebook, Instagram and Twitter; one page on sample messages and proposed ambassadors; and one page on financial commitment, ROI and deadlines.* (Timeframe) *Can you have a first draft to me next Friday?*

SMART outsourcing will literally take you a few minutes longer than SAT outsourcing, but this time investment is worth it – it will increase the prospect that the outsource service provider produces a great result the first time, minimising the amount of time (and cost) you spend on supervision and/or rework.

☑ Write down three ways you could use this strategy:

1. _____
2. _____
3. _____

☐ This strategy is a priority for me.
☐ I have implemented this strategy.

Insourcing At Home

Insourcing is the exact opposite of outsourcing. Insourcing is where you identify everything you do around the house for the people you live with that they can do for themselves and you don't have to pay them.

Regardless of your kids' ages, as long as they can walk there are tasks they can do around the house. The older your kids get, the more complex the tasks they can take on. And if your two year old can tidy away his/her toys then I'm pretty confident that your 40-year-old partner is capable of tidying up as well.

Without question, the younger you start your kids on insourcing the better – when they are young they are enthusiastic, compliant, tasks are a game, and they don't talk back. If you leave insourcing until your kids are teenagers you will be fighting a losing battle.

The key to insourcing is you are not after perfection – you simply want to instil in your family the habit of helping without a fight. Practice makes perfect.

'I live in a joint family home – it might sound a little bizarre to a lot of people – we have four generations staying in the same house. It is really lovely because the children can grow up with their grandparents and great-grandparents, cousins and aunties. There is always someone at home – so for instance if I am ever travelling I don't have to worry, and I can do my own things as well. My second tip is to have a good husband – we share responsibilities.'

Anu Acharya, CEO, MapMyGenome

The Five Time Investment Basics for SMART Insourcing are:

1. Family is a team sport. Sit down as a family and discuss who is going to do what.

2. Everyone is responsible for their own stuff and their own room – pack it up; put it away; clean it up; put the dirty stuff in the wash; put the clean stuff in the cupboard.

3. Identify the family-based tasks, divide them up and rotate them (so that no-one gets stuck permanently with the really bad jobs) – for example, feed the pets; walk the dog; take out the bins; vacuum the floor; pack and unpack the dishwasher.

4. Divide, conquer and teach – start your kids young. When they are little it's all about instilling good habits: no-one expects a six year old to vacuum like a pro. However, by the time s/he is 15 s/he will be a pro, and what's more, s/he won't argue when you hand over the vacuum, because family is, and always has been, a team sport.

5. Work together – this is family time. A great example of this is in the kitchen. Cook together. Your three year old can rip up the herbs, shake in the salt and pepper, and measure out a cup of flour. By the time your three year old is 10, s/he has had seven years' experience in the kitchen and will be cooking meals for the family.

'I married well. I have a very supportive husband who has pushed me across lots of different elements of my life. So when I wanted to really focus on different things, he stepped up to the plate in taking care of the kids and also the house and things like that. He's probably the primary chef at the moment and the primary laundry guy.

'I think getting the husbands on board is really important. And it's not asking permission because I've learned that sometimes when I ask for permission he says no, so it's kind of saying: "This is what I want to do and this is why I want to do it and I just want to make sure that you're okay with me doing it; and if you have any major objections to me doing it let me know."

'And often they don't have major objections – they may have little objections like: "Well what are we going to do if you're gone three nights a week?" and, "What are we going to do if...", but that is when you negotiate.

'But I think women often don't have the courage to say "This is what I want," and actually understanding that by getting what you want in a way that doesn't hurt the other person in the relationship, you're bound to be a better spouse and a better partner.'

Joy Foster, Founder and Managing Director, Tech Pixies

☑ Write down three ways you could use this strategy:

1. _____
2. _____
3. _____

☐ This strategy is a priority for me.
☐ I have implemented this strategy.

---

50 Jobs You Can Insource At Home

Here is a sample of the types of tasks you can insource at home:

The individual – it's your 'stuff', you deal with it – chores:

1. Clean up your floordrobe.
2. Hang up your towel (no, not like that…spread it out so that it dries).
3. Put your dirty clothes in the laundry basket: not on your floor, the bathroom floor, the living room floor, the kitchen floor, my bedroom floor or the car floor.
4. Put your clean clothes in your cupboard.
5. When I said clean up your floordrobe (see #1) that does not mean picking up all the clothes on your floor and putting them in the laundry. Half of that stuff is clean. Put the clean clothes in your cupboard and the dirty clothes in the wash.
6. Make your bed. Yes, it's okay if the doona is just lumped on the bed, as long as it's not on the floor.
7. Put your rubbish in the bin, not on your floor.
8. Flush the toilet.
9. Change the toilet roll.
10. Put the empty toilet roll in the bin, which is right next to the toilet for absolute convenience.
11. That same bin is also really handy for the empty toothpaste, empty hair products, balls of tissues and crusty band aids. Don't you just love a bin!
12. Put away your computer, phone, speaker, cords, earphones.

13. Put away your books, toys, cars, blocks, Lego, dolls, dress-ups.

14. Put away your hair ties, hair brush, hair products, hair dryer, hair straightener.

15. Put away your kinder bag, creche bag, library bag, school bag, school books, pencil case, school shoes.

16. Put away your sports clothes, cricket gear, lacrosse gear, football gear, soccer gear, swimming bag, dance gear, running gear, bike, bike helmet, surfboard, skateboard, scooter, pogo stick.

17. Put your dirty, wet, muddy, smelly, sports clothes in the laundry (see #3).

18. Put away your paints, paint brush, paintings, pencils, colouring books.

19. Put away your lipstick, foundation, blush, mascara, brushes, mirrors, eye liners, eyebrow pencils, eye lash curler, sponges, creams, sprays.

20. Put away your half-eaten food, dirty plates, dirty cups, forks, knives, spoons, straws, chocolate wrappers, lolly wrappers, ice-cream wrappers, chip packets, drink bottles.

21. Unpack your school bag, throw away the rubbish, throw away the old fruit at the bottom of the bag, wash your lunchbox, take out the school notes and give them to me, wipe out your bag because it smells.

22. Make your school lunch – there's lots of great food in the fridge, help yourself, it's not hard.

23. Make your snack – it's in the same place as the rest of the food.

24. Change your linen – honey you are 10, I think your arms are long enough to put a cover on the doona.

25. Get your own towel – look, here is a cupboard full of them.
26. Don't leave your rubbish in the car.

The family is a team sport buddy – deal with it chores:
27. Take the bins out.
28. Bring the bins in.
29. Wash the dishes.
30. Set the table.
31. Clear the table.
32. Mum…what's for dinner? I don't know honey, what are you cooking tonight?
33. Help cook dinner.
34. Feed the pets.
35. Clean up after the pets.
36. Walk the dog.
37. Vacuum the floor.
38. See this wet thing? It's called a mop. Please mop the kitchen.
39. Mow the lawn.
40. Sweep the leaves.
41. Put on a load of washing – that's okay, I'll show you how to use the washing machine. It's easy.
42. Put the washing out.
43. Bring the washing in.
44. Fold the washing.
45. Wipe down your shower.
46. Wipe out your sink.
47. Clean your toilet.

48. The shopping list is on the fridge; if you are the last to use something then (i) put it in the bin and (ii) add it to the shopping list.

49. Pack the dishwasher.

50. Unpack the dishwasher.

Be strong. From now on when you see your family's stuff lying around just begging you to pick it up/clear it away/tidy it/make it magically disappear, take a breath, kick it out of the way and shut the door so you don't have to look at it.

Remind your family about what they agreed to do.

Remind yourself that you are breaking two habits:

• The habits of your family members, who are used to leaving their 'stuff' lying around because they know you will pick it up and put it away.

• Your habit of picking it up and putting it away.

Who cares if you are the parent or partner who constantly reminds everyone to do their chores? It's better than being the parent or partner who constantly *does* all of the chores.

Susan Burton, Founder and CEO, Classlist.com

Susan Burton was living in India with her family when she registered the business name Classlist.com. Having relocated a number of times with her family, a problem she experienced in every new location was how difficult it was to meet other school parents. School contact lists were generally on spreadsheets and were pretty hit and miss. She knew there must be a better and quicker way for parents to connect with each other and help each other with the job of parenting.

SMART TIME INVESTMENT FOR BUSINESS

Susan had found a gap in the market, and she knew she could solve for it:

Someone said to me – 'Go and build it'. I had built websites before – I had built a social network site in India based on connecting expats, so I kind of pivoted that technology into this area and we just got traction.

Classlist.com is a secure web-based platform accessible to parents, providing class lists as well as a social platform for parents to connect, share drop offs and pick ups, trade and exchange goods, and set up events.

One of Susan's early challenges was how to manage the domestic load between herself and her husband while in start-up phase, when all of her attention was on the business:

Originally I tried to appeal to his empathy – 'Oh, I can't cope, it's all too much' – it simply did not register. And then I thought: 'I'm going about this completely wrong'. So then I went and did some research about domestic tasks and I got some UN data and pulled it all together. I worked out per square footage of house how many hours you should be spending on domestic tasks – an economic analysis of the division of labour – then I presented it to my husband and said: 'This is the situation with domestic tasks and how much time women spend and this is how much time men spend, and this is how much time per square footage of house we should be spending on different things'.

It wasn't emotional, it was just numbers.

I had a whole list and we ticked through who was going to do what and we made sure that it was even. He signed up to that.

I was very nice because I gave him cooking as I thought cooking is better than laundry – it's more fun and more satisfying – but then he failed to meet the service level agreement because there was no food on time!

He's now in charge of laundry. There was one occasion when the kids were saying: 'Where are my underpants? Where are my underpants?!' So he tried to do an express wash during breakfast and then iron them, and they were steaming. And I'm like: 'It's not my problem'.

I now have a backup plan – I buy five pairs of knickers and five pairs of socks a week in our online grocery shop. It's about managing mental load. Investing £5 a week on socks means I can reduce my mental load…that's how I get around that.

It's chaotic – but you just have to lower your standards!

'You can have it all, but only with the right support network. If you don't have the right support, it is impossible to make it work.'

Alexandra Depledge, Founder and CEO, Resi

☑ Write down three ways you could use this strategy:

1. _____
2. _____
3. _____

☐ This strategy is a priority for me.
☐ I have implemented this strategy.

A Half Hour Of Power

This one is a beauty for getting the house tidied quickly.

The Five Time Investment Basics for a Half Hour of Power are:

1. Family is a team sport – so get everyone in the house involved.

2. Allocate a room (or two) per person – this means they have to put everything in that room back where in belongs, plus run the vacuum over the floor of that room.

3. Choose your tunes and crank them up really loud. Rev the troops up: 'Go! GO! GOOO!' This is about getting maximum energy for half an hour – you want an absolute frenzy of activity.

4. Set the **timer (88)** for 30 minutes.

5. When the timer goes off, stop. You will have made a big dent in the chaos, so celebrate as a team and hang out together doing some fun stuff (a Want).

☑ Write down three ways you could use this strategy:

1. _____
2. _____
3. _____

☐ This strategy is a priority for me.
☐ I have implemented this strategy.

Shop Online

Shop online for everything. *Everything.*

Online shopping offers maximum convenience and saves you hours of time over the course of a year (seriously – for a single shopping trip, think of the time it takes for: the commute × 2; finding a car park; walking to the shops; walking around the shops; walking between shops; lining up for the register; loading the car; returning the trolley. Now multiply that by two or three trips a week and then by 52 weeks a year).

Embrace all things online; for example, supermarket shopping, business and school supplies, clothing (or at least clothing basics), banking and other money matters.

✍ Write down three ways you could use this strategy:

1. _____

2. _____

3. _____

☐ This strategy is a priority for me.
☐ I have implemented this strategy.

Rejects

You are operating at pace and your time is precious. You need to focus on what really matters and channel your energy into that, and reject the rest – it's just white noise.

Based on your **analysis (32)** of your **time maps (31)**, the tasks you performed across three days, and your categorisation of those tasks, highlight each of the tasks you have identified as being something you can potentially reject.

There are two types of Rejects:

- **Total Rejects:** the tasks no-one needs to perform because they are an absolute **waste of time (1)**.

- **Partial Rejects:** the tasks you do need to perform, but which you can be smarter about where, when, and how you do them. This book is full of strategies to help you do that.

☑ Write down three ways you could use this strategy:

1. _____
2. _____
3. _____

☐ This strategy is a priority for me.
☐ I have implemented this strategy.

'We give people permission here to walk out of meetings that are not productive. I think people have the right to control their own time. And if somebody decides to go off and do something on their phone in the middle of a meeting, that's okay. It is my fault for not being engaging enough.

'At Starling we take out of the schedule things that eat up your time: and people have meetings, get together, and disappear if it's not working.'

Anne Boden, CEO and Founder, Starling Bank

'At this time in my life, if I don't have bandwidth to do it, I don't.'
Susan Burton, Founder and CEO, Classlist.com

Deal With The Total Rejects

There is no justification at all to continue performing any task you have identified as a Total Reject. Discard your Total Rejects immediately – as in, today!

'I never really thought about Rejects until I started looking at your book [Me Time: The Professional Woman's Guide to finding 30 guilt-free hours a month]. *I think I have time for lots and lots of things… but if I actually look at my life and see how I find that time, I'm quite structured in how I eliminate from my schedule things that I don't have to do.'*
Anne Boden, CEO and Founder, Starling Bank

'I reject anything I hate to do that makes me… like, mad.

'At home I hate anything to do with the operations of how our kitchen works, and at work I hate booking people online. I would rather shoot myself in the head. I don't touch it.

'So I get in that really funny place where I pick up the phone and the caller will say – "Can you book me?", and I'm thinking, "Probably not. Probably not."'
Geeta Sidhu-Robb, CEO, Nosh Detox

'I think we have a very different relationship with our customers. What matters to us is listening to customers, talking to customers and building things that work for customers, and everything in the middle is a bit of a distraction. We don't do things that are internally focused. There's no point in having to spend a huge amount of time on a presentation for each other or for me – that's not for customers. So we really focus on things that are outward. We don't have lots of internal meetings. What really matters is that we work towards a goal.'

Anne Boden, CEO and Founder, Starling Bank

☑ Write down three ways you could use this strategy:

1. _____
2. _____
3. _____

☐ This strategy is a priority for me.
☐ I have implemented this strategy.

Create A 'Don't-Do List'

If you are finding the immediate rejection of your **Total Rejects (53)** challenging – after all, sometimes old habits die hard – start and maintain a list of your Total Rejects (essentially your 'don't-do list'). This is a running record of the habits and behaviours you no longer want to maintain. Keep your don't-do list handy and as a reminder that you are no longer going to do the dumb stuff, because now you know better. Continue to add to it as you identify other Total Rejects.

> *'Recognise that you don't have to do absolutely everything, and you can actually say: "I'm not going to do that". When I had to do big layoffs [in my business] I decided I was just going to strip my life of anything that was too much.*
>
> *'I was the governor at my children's school and my term just ended so I didn't renew the term; I was on a committee for a technology women's group here in Oxford and I told them: "I'm sorry, I can't do this anymore". I was in an entrepreneurs' group once a month so I dropped that too, and said to myself: "Anything that I can get off my schedule for now I just need to get it off – I need to stop networking for probably three or four months".*
>
> *'It's taken me a long time to figure out that you don't have as much time as you think. If you need to drop things temporarily in order to focus on what's important, do it.'*
>
> **Joy Foster**, Founder and Managing Director, Tech Pixies

☑ Write down three ways you could use this strategy:

1. _____
2. _____
3. _____

☐ This strategy is a priority for me.
☐ I have implemented this strategy.

SMART TIME INVESTMENT FOR BUSINESS

Reject Guilt

If you have any form of parental guilt about running and loving your business, stop **wasting your time (1)** and energy on such a negative, useless emotion.

Do you think you would feel better or less guilt if you had a job that you hated?

Holly Tucker MBE, Founder & Chief Inspirator at Not On The High Street, Founder of Holly & Co

Holly Tucker founded Not On The High Street – an online marketplace for artisanal and handmade products – from her kitchen table in 2006. She still owns the table – it's now her desk. She describes her own journey with guilt:

Mother's guilt is something I carried around with me while building Not On The High Street for over a decade. It was only after probably way too long – actually four, five, six years later when someone said to me: 'You're not going to get a gold star… no-one's going to give you a gold star for feeling this guilt. Actually no-one's even going to recognise it.' So I thought, as a logical business woman this was a bit of a nuts thing I was doing to myself and I decided to ditch it.

I decided to concentrate on the positive – the quality of time not the quantity of time that I was getting with my son. I couldn't get on the floor and play Thomas the Tank Engine with him, I wasn't very good at that, but what I was good at was listening to him, understanding his dreams, creating little funny business cards together, making his room an office next to my office. The things I could give him I gave him so much of it, to the point that he asked for a plaque which was 'Harry's Office' next to my office.

He's just turned 13 and I have just helped him set up his own business called Sugar Boy. I've helped him understand what profit and loss is, wholesale, marketing, how you have to get out of bed to actually run a business, and it has been the greatest honour.

And at the end of all of that, he has now decided that he's loved his life with me as a mum with a difference, a business woman, so much that he's decided he doesn't want to go to university and he wants to work with me, and I can't wait to work with my son for as long as he'll have me.

'When my kids were younger I always worked. I had my business and that never stopped.

'I really worried about how they would grow because I wasn't around that much and we always had help to take them to school. I really worried whether I would connect with them and would they like me.

'Now they are 13 and 15, and I see kids whose mothers stopped work to raise them and I see no difference. I didn't know that then. But now I'm okay.'

Maria Hatzistefanis, President/CEO, Rodial Group (Rodial, NIP+FAB)

'I sometimes feel a bit guilty, but not that guilty.'

Susan Burton, Founder and CEO, Classlist.com

'We're awful about mother's guilt. I've felt guilty ever since my daughter was born. I don't feel guilty anymore. The biggest change I made was to move to four days a week. For whatever reason I feel completely okay now and I feel that my daughter gets enough "mummy time".

'I used to get this feeling that I was guilty about being at work because I wasn't with her and when I was with her I felt guilty that I wasn't supporting the business. Now I don't feel either.

'I like to tell myself that she's seeing a strong woman going to work and being a role model, while still feeling loved and cherished.'

Alexandra Depledge, Founder and CEO, Resi

☑ Write down three ways you could use this strategy:

1. _____
2. _____
3. _____

☐ This strategy is a priority for me.
☐ I have implemented this strategy.

Deal With The Partial Rejects

On your **Don't Do List (54)** add your Partial Rejects and set a **deadline (86)** in your **calendar (96)** to develop a new, smarter, time-saving approach to these essential tasks.

Don't **fridge gaze (57)**	Do make a meal plan once a week, list the ingredients you need and then **shop (online) (51)** once
Don't keep your email open all day	Do **batch emails (106)**
Don't work on the hard stuff when tired	Do **batch your energy (101)**
Don't do anything in peak hour	Do what you can online and during off-peak hours

---

☑ Write down three ways you could use this strategy:

1. _____

2. _____

3. _____

☐ This strategy is a priority for me.
☐ I have implemented this strategy.

Reject Fridge Gazing

You know how this one goes – where you stand in front of the fridge for 10 minutes each morning and ask yourself: *what will we have for dinner tonight?*

Stop **wasting your time (1)**.

Once a week, sit down (include the people you live with) and write up a meal plan. Work out what meal you will have each night and who is the cook. At the same time, have someone checking the fridge and pantry to make sure you have all the ingredients you need for each meal, and write up a shopping list so that you only hit the shops (online) once.

> ☑️ Write down three ways you could use this strategy:
>
> 1. _____
> 2. _____
> 3. _____
>
> ☐ This strategy is a priority for me.
> ☐ I have implemented this strategy.

Reject Peak Hour

If there are tasks that you simply can't perform online for whatever reason and you need to be out and about then, at all costs, avoid peak hour: that's any time between 7.30 am and 9.30 am; between 3 pm and 4 pm (school pick up); and 5 pm to 6.30 pm. It's a jungle out there.

> ☑️ Write down three ways you could use this strategy:
>
> 1. _____
> 2. _____
> 3. _____
>
> ☐ This strategy is a priority for me.
> ☐ I have implemented this strategy.

Reject Ironing

Do not buy clothes that require ironing.

If you can't avoid having a few crisp white cotton shirts or a lovely silk number, then **outsource (43)** ironing – for a few dollars this is time and money well spent.

✒ Write down three ways you could use this strategy:

1. _____
2. _____
3. _____

☐ This strategy is a priority for me.
☐ I have implemented this strategy.

Reject Piling

File, don't pile.

✒ Write down three ways you could use this strategy:

1. _____
2. _____
3. _____

☐ This strategy is a priority for me.
☐ I have implemented this strategy.

Work/Life Integration

Work/life balance is a myth – you cannot hope to perfectly balance all of the many facets of your life by giving equal weight to your business priorities and to your life priorities at the same time. It simply can't be done.

You work and you love it. You have a life outside work and you love that too. You love to do lots of things. Often your business priorities cross over into home, or you take your business with you on the go while you juggle other commitments including your family, or you handle 'home stuff' while on the job.

No-one spends exactly equal amounts of time, joy or endeavour on their business life as they do on their non-business life. Your business is simply a part of life and life is a concoction of all of the various tasks and activities you perform each day.

So, don't **waste your time (1)** chasing the work/life balance dream. Instead, think about work/life integration – where you give yourself permission to spend your time where it is most needed (by you or others) at any given time. That might be in your business, with your family, pursuing personal development, or simply spending time on the other many elements of your life.

> *'I call it a constant juggle. I'm always trying to learn to be better. I feel there is no right way. It's about prioritising things in stages – at a point in time my family and training are a priority and so work takes a step back, and then the next week it will switch around. I can't fit everything in, so it just comes down to values and priorities.'*
>
> **Brant Garvey**, Paralympian and Motivational Speaker

'The most important thing is that you are never going to have a completely, extraordinarily, balanced life – you can't do everything – people tend to give you the flexibility you need if you let them know.'

Anu Acharya, CEO, MapMyGenome

'It's not about having equal leisure and equal business – that's "BS". Sometimes when I'm in the flow I'm working seven days, and that's just where I need to be and that's fine. There is no such thing as balance – it's not about creating balance.'

Tim Dwyer, Managing Director of Shirlaws Australia; Partner of BoB (Business of Brand) Group; creator of the Growth Metrics Program

'One of my highlights of family life is the weekly family huddle – it's run like an Unruly team meeting. We all come together at the weekend and go through our diaries for the following week so we all know who's doing what and where they need to be. If any decisions need to be made then that's the place that we make the decisions. It doesn't take too long – it's 15 minutes to half an hour tops. We do it over brunch and we generally catch a couple of things each time (for example, dentist appointments or school concerts that haven't made it into the diary!), so it saves a lot of pain during the week ahead.'

Sarah Wood, Co-Founder and Chair, Unruly

'I think it's tough, there's no point in denying it. I have three children and they all have different needs. The only way to manage the juggle is with really good time management. I do drop a ball sometimes. But my kids also understand that they benefit from that juggle – we have a good lifestyle and they

benefit from that and they know why I'm working so hard in my business.

'And I'm also quite good at just focusing on them. Last weekend we had a bank holiday here in the UK and we went to a festival for the weekend. We were stuck in a field for three days – no mobiles, nothing – and they got all my attention then. So it's swings and roundabouts.'

Cathy Hayward, Founder and CEO, Magenta

☑ Write down three ways you could use this strategy:

1. _____

2. _____

3. _____

☐ This strategy is a priority for me.
☐ I have implemented this strategy.

Free Up Space In Your Brain

Your brain is only capable of working for so long before it fatigues and needs a rest.

Research into brain function and learning advances every day. For example, current research indicates that during sleep your brain sheds information that is not regularly or frequently used by you – such as the more inconsequential memories from your childhood. It is theorised that this act of shedding is one way your brain frees up space for new information.

So, do yourself a favour and make some more room in your brain by getting information out of your head and onto paper or onto your computer, phone or tablet.

This will also help you:

- save an enormous amount of time and energy that you would otherwise waste on recall
- more objectively and more easily evaluate conflicting or multiple pieces of information
- ensure tasks are better prioritised
- streamline decision making.

And the act of writing or typing will help make the information stick, aiding retention.

📝 Write down three ways you could use this strategy:

1. _____
2. _____
3. _____

☐ This strategy is a priority for me.
☐ I have implemented this strategy.

Manage Your Passwords

How many passwords do you have? Odds on it's 20-plus. And in a data-rich, privacy-sensitive, high-risk-of-being-hacked world, you want to make sure that each of your passwords is unique and hard to crack.

Do not **waste your time (1)** trying to remember all these different passwords – **free up space in your brain (62)** and also make for a more productive day by using a password management tool. Your computer or device may already have built-in password management, or there are many options available online for little or no cost. You will no longer have to worry about remembering all your passwords, and many of these tools will also sync your passwords across all of your devices.

☑ Write down three ways you could use this strategy:

1. _____
2. _____
3. _____

☐ This strategy is a priority for me.
☐ I have implemented this strategy.

Reject Perfectionism

While it's important to plan, it's also important to *do*. Don't aim for perfection. You don't have the time, or frankly the need, to be perfect. Know when good enough is more than enough. Aiming for perfection takes a lot more time, with little or no additional benefit to your business.

> *'You can be far more productive with your time when you realise that a lot of the time you're trying to decide between something that is 95% right with Option A and 97% right with Option B. I'm not going to spend my time worrying about that – they're both good options.'*
>
> **Anne Boden**, CEO and Founder, Starling Bank

'You just have to start. What most people do, and I definitely fell victim to this, is that you want to be prepared so you do lots of research and speak to lots of people and read lots of things, and actually you just need to jump in and start. Just do something. Less talking, more action.'

Alexandra Depledge, Founder and CEO, Resi

'In traditional organisations what you normally do is you build something and the build process takes a long time. First of all you decide what the budget is; then you decide on the Steering Committee; and then you all get together to agree something; and then you draw a long plan; and you're really worried about missing the date so you set a lot of key meetings; and you think about contingency. And then, in the end, you have the plan.

'Perhaps a couple of percent is actually doing the work and the rest is actually planning to do the work! So what we do [at Starling Bank] is we just do the work and we do it very quickly, and instead of lots of hierarchies and lots of structures, people are very self-organising.

'We just do things.'

Anne Boden, CEO and Founder, Starling Bank

📝 Write down three ways you could use this strategy:

1. _____

2. _____

3. _____

☐ This strategy is a priority for me.
☐ I have implemented this strategy.

Evaluate Your Decisions

Understand the difference between simple and complex decisions and adjust your time commitment accordingly.

How much time do you really need to spend on each decision you make?

> ☑ Write down three ways you could use this strategy:
> 1. _____
> 2. _____
> 3. _____
> ☐ This strategy is a priority for me.
> ☐ I have implemented this strategy.

Make (Simple) Decisions Fast

Do not agonise over simple decisions. Make simple decisions quickly and then pivot on the go if required.

Simple decisions include, for example:

- what to wear (have a uniform look)
- what to eat (have a list of what you like and make sure that you always stock it)

- whether to exercise (yes, it's good for your body and your brain)
- when to go to bed and when to get up (have standard times and stick to them)
- allocate a place where you always put your keys, phone, wallet, charger, pens, and so on, so that you don't waste time or mental energy looking for them every single day.

Identify the simple decisions; make them; and then move on.

'At Starling we do things very, very quickly.

'When I hire I interview people and it's very quick. There's no need to talk to somebody for 30 minutes if in 10 minutes you know. So we are very quick because we have to be very frugal with our time.'

Anne Boden, CEO and Founder, Starling Bank

☑ Write down three ways you could use this strategy:

1. _____
2. _____
3. _____

☐ This strategy is a priority for me.
☐ I have implemented this strategy.

SMART TIME INVESTMENT FOR BUSINESS

Make (Simple) Decisions Once

You've made the decision, so don't keep re-making it. That is a complete **waste of your time** (1). If you decide you are going to exercise every morning, for example, then that is your decision. Do not rethink that decision every single day when the alarm goes off.

'We just do things. Traditionally in a bank you'd be putting out new releases every three months or something, but we do new releases several times a day. Instead of saving up all those changes and planning a big release and launching it to the public, we do the opposite. Every day we put four or five little things live and that means the risk of something going wrong is very, very small.'

Anne Boden, CEO and Founder, Starling Bank

☑ Write down three ways you could use this strategy:

1. _____

2. _____

3. _____

☐ This strategy is a priority for me.
☐ I have implemented this strategy.

Make (Complex) Decisions Slowly

For more complex, important decisions, take the time to evaluate your options and make slower, well-informed decisions.

While it is important to acknowledge and trust your gut, for the more complex or important decisions, gut-based decisions are not enough. While your instinct may be pointing you in a certain direction, your gut is acting on muscle memory – reverting to a more emotional and subconsciously biased way of making decisions. Ultimately it '*feels right*' because your brain remembers that this is the way you have dealt with a particular choice in the past.

A gut-based decision alone, for more complex decisions, is like flipping a coin – you will win some and you will lose some. To tip the balance towards more wins, stress test your gut against a well reasoned decision-making **process (27)**. A decision-making process will include answering questions such as:

- What type of options will I evaluate?

- What criteria will I assess each option against?

- What data will I rely on?

- Who will I consult with?

You can save an enormous amount of time, and angst, by having a written decision-making process that you revert to each time you are faced with a more complex decision.

✏️ Write down three ways you could use this strategy:

1. _____
2. _____
3. _____

☐ This strategy is a priority for me.
☐ I have implemented this strategy.

Create A Great Morning Routine

Establish a morning routine that makes you feel great, and then stick to it; for example, get up at the same time each day; exercise; eat well; meditate; focus; and then start work.

Start your work day like you have already won.

Chris Robb, Founder and CEO, Mass Participation Asia

Chris Robb is a 30-year veteran of the mass-participation sports industry. His first business, Spectrum Worldwide, delivered some of Asia's largest mass-participation sports events, including the Standard Chartered Marathon Singapore (55,000 runners) and Cycle Asia that attracts nearly 25,000 cyclists to events in Singapore, Malaysia, Philippines and Australia. Chris sold Spectrum Worldwide to IRONMAN in 2016, and founded his current business, Mass Participation Asia. There are few people globally with Chris's depth and breadth of knowledge in the mass-participation sports industry.

My most important time investment tip is to have a powerful morning ritual that gets you on a roll and in the zone.

I am absolutely most productive in the morning, and that is because I have a powerful morning ritual including Wim Hof breathing; energy activation; journaling; and exercise. My ritual sets me up to be focused and productive. I'm also lucky to have a wonderful workspace that allows me to hear the early morning sounds of nature, which I love.

I find almost without fail that the days when I am less productive and manage my time poorly are those days where I was not able to do my morning ritual. Strong evening rituals are equally important to review the day and set myself up for the following one.

'*I find I work best in the mornings because I begin my day with quiet time to clear my head and, as an aromatherapist, I love inhaling essential oils to help with process. It's kind of like a mini-meditation.*'

Catherine Cervasio, Director, ALUXE Pty Ltd

☑ Write down three ways you could use this strategy:

1. _____
2. _____
3. _____

☐ This strategy is a priority for me.
☐ I have implemented this strategy.

Piggy Back Good Habits

A simple, but effective strategy to help make a new, good time habit sticky is to piggy back the new habit off an existing good habit. For example, you may be in the habit of reaching for your phone the minute you wake up to check your messages. This is a bad time habit. Your new good time habit will see you **batch device usage (105)** to a later point in the morning.

If that feels a little hard right now, piggy back breaking your early morning device addiction to a good habit; for example, the habit of showering in the morning (a good habit). Tomorrow, and the next day, and the next, and until the new habit sticks, as you roll over to reach for your phone, think: *No – it's time to have a shower.*

☑ Write down three ways you could use this strategy:

1. _____

2. _____

3. _____

☐ This strategy is a priority for me.
☐ I have implemented this strategy.

Respond Don't React

We live and work in a fast-paced business world where many of our communications with our customers, prospects and suppliers occur online.

One of the upsides of this is that it often speeds up our working interactions. One of the downsides is that device-driven communications are devoid of body language and vocal intonation which help guide how well our information is received and processed. This leaves online communications, which are often quite succinct in their nature to begin with, very open to interpretation. One person's 'brief and to the point' might be another person's 'abrupt, rude and confrontational'.

Be conscious of this, both in sending and receiving information online.

The Five Time Investment Basics for Sending Online Communications are:

1. No knee-jerk reactions. If in doubt, draft the communication and sit on it for an hour or two before sending.
2. Write the way you talk: start with a greeting or pleasantry and end with a standard closing.
3. Have a clear purpose *(what do I need?)* and be short and to the point to save time and to avoid confusion.
4. Put yourself in the recipient's shoes *(how will these words be read?)*.
5. Proofread before you send.

☑ Write down three ways you could use this strategy:

1. _____
2. _____
3. _____

☐ This strategy is a priority for me.
☐ I have implemented this strategy.

Define Success Early

You started your business because you had a great idea for a product(s) or service(s) that you believe people will be prepared to pay for, because it solves a problem.

SMART TIME INVESTMENT FOR BUSINESS

But does it really solve a problem? And will people be prepared to pay for it? And if so, how much will they pay? And if so, how many people? And who are your major competitors? And…

Prior to launching your business or new product or service, you need to have a very clear idea of what success looks like and you need to be able to articulate that. Why? Because once you launch you will be working at pace, with a huge number of 'to-do's' and competing priorities to address. Moreover, having a predetermined, clear and rationally thought out picture of what success looks like – that also indicates without emotion if and when it's time to shut down an idea and move on to the next one – will save you a lot of time, heartache and money.

> 'In the early days of Unruly, before we launched the video advertising marketplace, we tried out lots of different business models, including a comedy website, a viral video chart and a video analytics tool.

> 'In the start, the amount of time we devoted to new ideas massively varied because some ideas were big, some were small, some you could test in 24 hours, some took a week or two; but we're talking weeks rather than months for testing cycles. And that's still the case now. When Unruly launches a new product or feature we launch an MVP (minimum viable product) so we can get client feedback at the earliest opportunity, and we constantly measure traction and monitor feedback so we can start iterating and improving the proposition.

> 'It can be difficult sunsetting products, so I'd suggest being tough on yourself. I think it's always a good idea to define your test and set out your metrics for success (I like good/better/best scenarios)

before *you get underway and before you have too much emotional attachment to the idea.*

'One of the mistakes I see entrepreneurs make is not being clear enough about success metrics early enough in the process, and by the time they start defining success metrics they're already quite emotionally invested in the idea and skewing what success looks like because they don't want to give up on their "baby".

'Once you've come up with your idea, start defining success metrics straight off the bat, just with your intuition. In the first three months, is it success if we have 100 users? Or is it success if we have 1000 users? I've always thought that orders of magnitude are a good place to start when you don't have access to mounds of data.'

Sarah Wood, Co-Founder and Chair, Unruly

☑ Write down three ways you could use this strategy:

1. _____
2. _____
3. _____

☐ This strategy is a priority for me.
☐ I have implemented this strategy.

Test And Measure

You can only gauge **success (72)** by constantly testing, measuring and understanding the potential of your business.

Schedule regular time into your **calendar (96)** to measure the financial performance of:

- the business as a whole
- current product and service offerings
- leads
- customer satisfaction
- customer retention
- market share.

And there are many other metrics you can measure as well. Work out what data you need to make good decisions, and analyse this data often.

'We've become better at identifying a single test and measuring it as we've gone along but it still takes discipline.'
Sarah Wood, Co-Founder and Chair, Unruly

'You need to measure what's actually happening today before you can change tomorrow.

'To know the potential of your business, you need to know the potential of each of your products. If you don't know how to measure the potential of each existing product, you risk not leveraging each product to its full capacity.

'I see a lot of business owners jumping in and developing new products before they have reached the potential of their current product line. They essentially waste a lot of their time and money building out new products that they didn't even need.

'Knowing the capacity of your products and services allows you to focus your time on maximising your existing assets. Then, once you have maximised existing assets, you can focus on new assets to grow your business.

'You can't know where to spend your time or plan for business growth until you have measured the potential of your business.'

Tim Dwyer, Managing Director of Shirlaws Australia; Partner of BoB (Business of Brand) Group; creator of the Growth Metrics Program

---

☑ Write down three ways you could use this strategy:

1. _____
2. _____
3. _____

☐ This strategy is a priority for me.
☐ I have implemented this strategy.

Perseverance And Resilience

Perseverance and resilience are learned skills. As a business owner you demonstrate these skills with your ability to keep getting up, and keep going, every time you are knocked down.

When you think perseverance and resilience, think Rocky Balboa: *'You, me, or nobody is gonna hit as hard as life. But it ain't about how hard you hit. It's about how hard you can get hit and keep moving forward; how much you can take and keep moving forward. That's how winning is done.'*

Here are three other lessons Rocky has to teach business owners about perseverance and resilience:

1. *'Every champion was once a contender that refused to give up':* You have already defied the odds by striking out on your own without the safety net that comes with having a regular corporate job and a consistent sum of money hitting your bank account each fortnight. None of this would have been possible if you weren't a self-sufficient, passionate, driven, and unstoppable legend.

2. *'Nothing is real if you don't believe in who you are':* Ultimately, if you don't believe in yourself and your business then what's the point? Be true to your values and don't compromise on what is most important to you.

3. *'The world ain't all sunshine and rainbows':* Business isn't a popularity contest – not everyone is going to love what you do. But you want the people who do love what you do to love you vehemently. That can't occur if you aren't polarising the market. Don't settle for being vanilla and running a vanilla business just so people like you. No-one ever changed the world with vanilla.

Brant Garvey, Paralympian and Motivational Speaker

Brant Garvey was the first Australian above-knee amputee to compete in an Ironman Triathlon (3.8 km swim, 180 km ride, 42 km run), setting a world-record time in the process. As a motivational speaker, Brant's passion for sports and fitness is equalled only by his desire to educate and inspire others to lead their greatest possible life:

One skill I'm more passionate about is resilience – which comes from having setbacks over my life and having to overcome those with my

142

disability. And in the world of elite sport there is just setback after setback. It's the same in the business world – you have to be able to adapt. And the quicker you can adapt then the quicker you can regain traction.

'It was always my dream to get my products into Harvey Nicholls – it is an exclusive store, all the best designers are there, all the big brands, but it is also very boutique.

'After succeeding with my first store, I thought: it must be easy, I will send them an email and a bunch of products. But it wasn't easy. They would either not respond to my email or they would send an email saying: "I'm really sorry but we do not have space for you".

'I would get very disappointed, take some time off and look into other accounts, and then a year later I would try again. I would send them some new products, press we had achieved, an update, and hope to get a meeting.

'And that kept on happening for seven years, to the point where I thought: "We are never going to get into that store!" But, you know, until I get an email from someone saying, "Stop emailing us! You are dead to us!", I would very politely connect. Obviously you don't want to be a stalker so I would give it a year and make sure I had some progress to show, and I would be very respectful and share information.

'And it took me seven years.

'Sometimes getting a No is disheartening, but with me it really drives me to work harder and be better and to turn this No into a Yes one day.

'I was very proud to get our products into Harvey Nicholls. And this is the store that actually supported us with our first flagship counter a few years later.

'Things will be okay in the end. If you persevere things will work out. You face challenges every day. Have a long-term view, a vision, and don't worry about the day-to-day problems at the start.'

Maria Hatzistefanis, President/CEO, Rodial Group (Rodial, NIP+FAB)

'We are often so hard on ourselves and judge ourselves so harshly, and when we do that, we hold ourselves back.'

Tim Dwyer, Managing Director of Shirlaws Australia; Partner of BoB (Business of Brand) Group; creator of the Growth Metrics Program

'Falling is part of the journey. Own it. But then let it go. Because the fall shouldn't be the focus – what you choose to do next is the focus. Whatever happens, it's only a setback if you quit. So, pick yourself up and keep going because there is no better way to prepare for tomorrow – the next fall but also the next success – than to challenge yourself today.'

Brant Garvey, Paralympian and Motivational Speaker

Write down three ways you could use this strategy:

1. _____
2. _____
3. _____

☐ This strategy is a priority for me.
☐ I have implemented this strategy.

Fail Fast

If your business idea, or new product or service idea, is not going to be successful then you want it to fail as quickly as possible. Failing fast saves time and money.

This is not about personal failure, this is about learning and evolving. It's about what's good for your business. You want to get the failures out of the way as quickly as possible so that you can spend your time on the successes.

'Don't be afraid to fail. It's how you get to the right answer.'
Michelle Kennedy, Co-Founder and CEO, Peanut

'I have made a success out of failing and moving on. I've never worried about it. Actually, I have to say I'm always telling the children that. I just don't see that failing at something makes me a failure, and I've had to really clearly identify that because, of course, I'm Indian and failing at anything made me a failure because that was my upbringing. And in order to survive I had to really understand that distinction, and I had to understand that failing was in itself a form of success.'
Geeta Sidhu-Robb, CEO, Nosh Detox

'If you haven't failed and you are trying to raise money [in Silicon Valley] they will look down on you. They say: "Why would we trust our money with you if you haven't gone and experimented

and tried to give this a go and failed? You are a much higher risk for us." It's really important – you won't raise as much money as you want if you haven't failed.'

Susan Burton, Founder and CEO, Classlist.com

'I almost feel like people should do a business and fail as quickly as possible so they can do the second one, because it feels so infinitely easier than the first.'

Alexandra Depledge, Founder and CEO, Resi

☑️ Write down three ways you could use this strategy:

1. _____

2. _____

3. _____

☐ This strategy is a priority for me.
☐ I have implemented this strategy.

Learn, Unlearn, Then Learn Some More

You don't know everything. And lots of the stuff you do know is no longer relevant. And lots of the stuff you do know is still relevant but just in a different way. And then there is a lot of new stuff that you don't even know that you don't know, but that you really do need to know.

First, take the time to be and stay digitally aware. The exponential rate of technological advancement means you need to keep up, and keep on keeping up. Invest time in ongoing digital learning – stay apace with technology and adapt your business and your business processes to take advantage of the productivity and efficiency gains technology brings.

Second, commit the time to hone the skills you have which can't easily be replicated by technology, such as creativity, logic, problem solving, agility, adaptability, relationship management, and resilience. This is where your business differentiation lies.

Third, learn from your mistakes – understand what went wrong, when it when wrong, how you could have dealt with the situation differently, and what you will and won't do next time.

You will need to learn and unlearn and then learn some more. Forever.

'You just have to keep on trying things; when they don't work out you try something different. You learn by doing when you're an entrepreneur. Especially if you're a tech founder or a pioneer in your field, there is no textbook telling you what to do.'
Sarah Wood, Co-Founder and Chair, Unruly

Alexandra Depledge, Founder and CEO, Resi

Alexandra Depledge has form for setting up businesses that solve for her own problems. Her first business, hassle.com, was co-founded in London in 2013 and became a phenomenally successful home-cleaning online booking service across Europe, eventually selling for £27 million.

Her second, and current, business Resi solves another typical home-based problem – helping home owners complete building projects by scouring residential codes to assess whether a new building design is viable, costing the project and providing initial architectural concept and designs.

Reflecting on her first business, Alexandra recalls the entire journey as incredibly amazing on the one hand and rather traumatic on the other, and she was determined to take the lessons she learnt into her second business venture:

It was two-and-a-half years from start to finish – from figuring out the model to selling it. To put that in context, there were five of us [in the business] for the whole of 2013 when we relaunched the product. And then between January 2014 and March 2014 we raised $6 million. And then I fell pregnant and didn't realise it until about May. But in that space between March and May 2014 we hired 35 people, so from 5 [people] to 35 [people] in the space of eight weeks, to 100 [people] in another space of eight weeks to four countries by the end of the year.

I don't know what we thought we were doing – it was just too fast. We never caught our breath. We were always fighting fires. We were never doing anything proactively. That was traumatic enough without having a kid in the middle of it!

And then I had my child on 1 February [2015], and on 4 February we started to acquire a German company. By March I was on a flight to Munich, and shortly after that we started getting acquisition offers.

So to do all of that in the space of less than 2.5 years, it was a great experience and I learnt on speed if you like, but it was phenomenally intense. When I came out the back end of that it was almost like I had PTSD. I got hugely depressed for a good four weeks. I was in a very dark place because hassle.com was my identity – it was this thing that I had nurtured – it was like my first baby. And letting it go I found really, really hard. It was a really difficult process, and then I had this little baby in the middle of it all that I didn't really know because I hadn't really seen her, she had been looked after by a nanny. And I had to process all of this stuff. I went into a really dark place and I had to claw my way out of it.

Part of that journey was asking: 'What do I need to change to make sure I never fall into that trap again?'

'When we have capability – the skill set to do something – it allows us to get into flow. But when we don't have capability, we feel uncomfortable because it is uncomfortable learning something new. People don't like being uncomfortable, so rather than leaning in and learning a new skill, we switch away from the new and we revert to what we already know.

'And when you revert back to what you already know, you won't grow your business.

'Business growth is all about building new capabilities – about continuing to learn. You need to work out what the capabilities are that you don't have and that you need to build and then you need lean into it. You need to go through the discomfort of learning the new skill. Once you are through the discomfort, the

new skill becomes a habit and you have shifted your business to a new level.'

Tim Dwyer, Managing Director of Shirlaws Australia; Partner of BoB (Business of Brand) Group; creator of the Growth Metrics Program

---

☑ Write down three ways you could use this strategy:

1. _____

2. _____

3. _____

☐ This strategy is a priority for me.
☐ I have implemented this strategy.

Invest In Learning

Often professionals who work in corporate take their ongoing access to learning and development for granted. When you own and run your own business, you need to curate your learning and development opportunities yourself.

Each year, take the time and allocate budget to your continuous professional and personal development. Go after both hard and soft skills. Your business will only continue to excel if you continue to grow and to innovate. The moment you stop learning is the moment your business stops growing.

'Women [in particular] do not invest in themselves. They don't understand their value and their worth and they don't feel that

they have the right to invest in themselves. This is a concept that I just had no understanding of whatsoever.'

Joy Foster, Founder and Managing Director, TechPixies

'Your business will only grow to the extent you are prepared to grow. That is the bottom line of everything – it is the start, the end, the up and the down.'

Geeta Sidhu-Robb, CEO, Nosh Detox

'I have an Executive Coach and it's the best money we spend as a company. When you are the CEO, nobody comes in and says: "You did really well today. Or you could do better", and actually everybody really needs that, especially the company needs that.'

Alexandra Depledge, Founder and CEO, Resi

'You need to take personal responsibility for implementing what you learn. Don't expect anything in life to "just work" without personal effort – your pen does not work until you pick it up and write with it – recognise that nothing works until you make it work.'

Glen Carlson, Co-Founder, Dent Global

☑ Write down three ways you could use this strategy:

1. _____

2. _____

3. _____

☐ This strategy is a priority for me.
☐ I have implemented this strategy.

Embrace Keyboard Shortcuts

If you spend a lot of time at your computer, learn and embrace keyboard shortcuts. If you can save just a few seconds each time you perform a task at your keyboard, over time the time savings will be huge.

> ☑ Write down three ways you could use this strategy:
>
> 1. _____
> 2. _____
> 3. _____
>
> ☐ This strategy is a priority for me.
> ☐ I have implemented this strategy.

Surround Yourself With The Right People

Running a business can be very isolating – especially when you first launch. It will be you, your brain, your great idea and, if you are lucky, a supportive family and friendship group there to cheer you on.

This is great, but this is not enough.

To save yourself a lot of time you need more than a core group of cheerleaders. In the next few strategies we'll look at the people you need on your team.

'Being an entrepreneur can be lonely. That's why it is so critical to surround yourself with the right people from day one – the people who will help you work smarter. And have the courage to turn to them during strife and pressure. A problem shared is a problem halved – I truly believe that.'

Chris Robb, Founder and CEO, Mass Participation Asia

'Surrounding yourself with the right people has a 100% impact on your ability to be successful.'

Brant Garvey, Paralympian and Motivational Speaker

☑ Write down three ways you could use this strategy:

1. _____

2. _____

3. _____

☐ This strategy is a priority for me.
☐ I have implemented this strategy.

Find The Right Business Mentors

Business mentors will help steer you and your business in the right direction. Choose mentors who have already blazed a trail, who you respect, and who you can tap into for advice and expertise beyond your own skill set. A great mentor can also connect you with other advisers, prospects and opportunities.

The Five Time Investment Basics for Choosing the Right Mentors are:

1. Don't limit yourself to one mentor. No one person can give you all the advice and guidance you will need.

2. Identify business leaders and subject matter experts with skill sets to complement your own areas of expertise.

3. You don't need to know the mentor before you approach her/ him. Look for common connections, leverage your network and ask for an introduction, or send a handwritten note (not an email – you need to differentiate yourself from the crowd).

4. Agree the ground rules up front: how often will you meet or connect? How formal or informal will the meetings be? What do you want from the relationship? What do they want from the relationship (generally mentors are happy to give their time to others, but it's important to try to make any business relationship a win–win)?

5. Don't be afraid to ask for what you need.

Anu Acharya, CEO, MapMyGenome

Anu Acharya is a leading entrepreneur and former Young Global Leader (World Economic Forum 2011). Her first business, Ocimum Bio Solutions, was one of India's fastest growing life sciences companies.

Concerned with the reactive rather than the preventative way healthcare is often practised, especially in India *(you fall sick and you go to the doctor, and sometimes you go too late)*, Anu was inspired to make genome assessment directly accessible to consumers. Her second company, MapMyGenome, is a molecular diagnostics company whose flagship product provides a personal genetic profile directly to the public, who can access the genome service online.

Anu's father, a physicist, was her first mentor:

When I was growing up, every summer from about the fifth grade my dad used to interview me about what I wanted to be. I would say: 'I want to be a physicist', because at that point, that was the limit of my universe. When I decided to change and become an entrepreneur, my dad was extraordinarily supportive – he said: 'You need to do something you want to do and I am not the one who is going to stop you.'

It's always helpful to have mentors, especially people who are likely to give you a different perspective to your own – someone who has gone on a different path, who can offer you complementary skills. My advisers are typically people who haven't had the same journey as me, but who are able to give me some perspective – they have built businesses. It is more about getting those kinds of people to give you advice on how they would look at the business from a completely different angle. And just the journey itself – someone who has gone through a similar journey.

'No-one gets to be successful without guidance. Successful people get information from others at every stage of the journey. They ask lots of questions and are inquisitive as to how people got to where they are. The best way to learn is to start with the premise that you don't know rather than you do. This way you will listen for the missing pieces of information rather than confirming what you already know.'

Tim Dwyer, Managing Director of Shirlaws Australia; Partner of BoB (Business of Brand) Group; creator of the Growth Metrics Program

'I'm a massive fan of both being mentored and being a mentor – I devote time each week to mentoring others. In my early years my mentors were more accidental than strategic, but I have been fortunate to have had some amazing mentors who have played a key role in my life. Surround yourself with a great group of mentors.'

Chris Robb, Founder and CEO, Mass Participation Asia

'I am a big believer in having business mentors, however I have really only brought mentors into my life over the past several years. I particularly like bouncing ideas off male mentors who, in my experience, often view situations differently to women. If I find a business decision a little overwhelming, it's great to chat to one of my mentors and see it from a different angle – using a different thought process.'

Catherine Cervasio, Director, ALUXE Pty Ltd

Write down three ways you could use this strategy:

1. _____
2. _____
3. _____

☐ This strategy is a priority for me.
☐ I have implemented this strategy.

Find Your Posse

Just because you are working alone, or with a partner, or with a small team, does not mean that you are on your own.

Take the time to find your posse – a diverse cohort of terrific business owners you can bounce ideas off; learn from; share wins and losses with; and partner and collaborate with. Diversity is key – you can't make the best decisions in your business unless you surround yourself with the best ideas from different perspectives using the best rigour.

Your posse will inspire you, drive you to greater heights, be there to celebrate the wins and to help you nut out the lessons when you fail. The right posse will provide an early testing ground, will give you honest and open feedback, will keep you accountable, and will help you cut through faster, better and smarter than if you do it on your own.

Make the time to find your posse.

Claire Davenport, CEO, HelloFresh UK

Claire Davenport is CEO of HelloFresh UK, the country's largest meal kit company and subsidiary of HelloFresh Group, named the fastest growing start-up in Europe over the past five years. Her focus is on continuously developing a customer-centric business that changes the way people eat, forever. With an extensive background of successfully scaling businesses and disrupting markets, Claire has been part of the executive team of a broad range of disruptor and tech brands over the past decade, including as Chief Commercial Officer at global online games company Bigpoint

GmbH, part of the launch team at online education company FutureLearn, and Chief of Staff at Skype. Prior to this, Claire was Executive Vice President of Strategy and Online at Europe's largest broadcasting company, RTL Group, sitting on the boards of subsidiaries Fremantle Media, Channel 5 (UK) and RTL Netherlands.

I have a group of female friends who lead internet companies, whom I have met through various industry events. We exchange notes, advice and contacts and meet up regularly. They are a brilliant network who support and advise through good times and bad, help make me a better leader, are a great source of opportunities and contacts in the market, and generally make life more fun.

'Don't underestimate the importance of a network. I never really understood it. I now know how important it is to find people along the way who are instrumental some way in your journey. You obviously have to pay it forward – you have to help them too, but there will be people that you meet along your life's journey who will be so instrumental in how you develop your career and what you decide to do, and that will start really early, and I don't think I ever really appreciated that.'

Michelle Kennedy, Co-Founder and CEO, Peanut

'If I have a problem I go and talk to my peer group.'
Susan Burton, Founder and CEO, Classlist.com

'Have an amazing community – non-judgemental colleagues from across the world who are willing to help you or listen to you.

I belong to a number of communities – each one offers a different perspective and a different value. I would recommend that every entrepreneur have a community they belong to – where you can talk about your challenges.'

Anu Acharya, CEO, MapMyGenome

'*Having a network isn't enough. There are a lot of groups where people just get together and talk about their problems. But, if there's no-one in the room that is an expert in the solution, then all they're doing is trying to solve a problem with the same thinking that created it.*

'*You have to have people around you that understand how to solve the problem – you need a network that's got the experts as well as the people that have got the motivation to actually get up and get stuff done.*

'*If someone can't articulate why the problems exist in the first place and then list out all the components, be a little careful of their advice as it might just be an idea of what to "try" rather than a proven path.'*

Tim Dwyer, Managing Director of Shirlaws Australia; Partner of BoB (Business of Brand) Group; creator of the Growth Metrics Program

---

📝 Write down three ways you could use this strategy:

1. _____

2. _____

3. _____

☐ This strategy is a priority for me.
☐ I have implemented this strategy.

Learn From Big Business

Identify early the behaviours and habits you want to instil in your business to power up – as opposed to stifle – productivity.

At all costs, you want to avoid the big business concept of organisational drag – where you lose time as a business as a result of the procedures, behaviours and operating rhythm embedded in your business. On average, big business loses more than 20% of its productive capacity – one day every working week – to organisational drag.

Big business is now looking to small business to identify the behaviours and culture that start-ups, in particular, create and perpetuate, which foster speed to market, agility, quick decision making, collaboration and high **productivity (4)**. This look over the fence is hardly surprising given most big businesses continue to operate on a business model developed over 200 years ago: a model which is supremely hierarchical and therefore slow to make decisions and innovate; with an annual set and forget financial budgeting mentality; and static job descriptions.

Do not make this mistake.

Instead, flip this learning around and look to big business for the behaviours and culture that you absolutely want to avoid instilling in your business. Consciously implement highly productive **business protocols (83)** and working habits from the outset, which you then regularly revisit, **measure (73)** and adapt to ensure that you stay focused on productive outcomes.

☑ Write down three ways you could use this strategy:

1. _____
2. _____
3. _____

☐ This strategy is a priority for me.
☐ I have implemented this strategy.

Create Business Protocols

Having **learnt from big business (82)**, establish a suite of simple business protocols that set the tone for how you want to invest your time – and the behaviours and culture you want to foster – in your business. Build these protocols around the business practices, habits and behaviours that will power up productivity. For example, consider:

1. **Meeting management (119)** : who can call a meeting; how often do you need to meet; what do you need to meet about; how long will your meetings generally be; who needs to be invited to meetings? *(Note: employees in big business spend up to two days a week in needless meetings, 80% of which occur within single departments – don't allow this.)*

2. **Email management (106)** : when will you deal with emails; how long will you spend on emails; if you have a team, is this the best way to communicate? *(Note: employees in big business spend 16 hours per week reading and responding to emails – don't allow this.)*

3. **Interruptions** (124) : how is your working space configured; does it foster or inhibit collaboration or interruptions; what interruptions will you allow and dismiss? *(Note: on average, professionals are interrupted 10 times an hour – don't allow this.)*

☑ Write down three ways you could use this strategy:

1. _____
2. _____
3. _____

☐ This strategy is a priority for me.
☐ I have implemented this strategy.

Create Time Budgets

As a business owner you rightly focus on financial budgets and a range of financial measures that track, in real time, the financial performance of your business. Your intent is to ensure the greatest possible financial return. As such, you only ever invest your money with an overarching strategic business plan, supported by controls that rigorously track and measure your expenditure and your return on your investment.

But what of your time? Are you also investing your time with the same level of intent and control for the greatest possible return? Probably not.

And yet, your time is money.

Consider establishing a time budget to sit alongside your financial budget. Your time budget should clearly identify where you plan to spend your time over the course of the coming year, and how much time you will invest in each type of task.

Break your time budget into different task categories and colour code these for simple reference in your calendar – this way you, and your team if you have one, can see at a glance where you are and should be spending your time (see **colour code your calendar (97)**).

If you have a team, their time budget will be different to yours and will be dictated by the role they perform. Actively monitor your own and your team's compliance with the time budgets and adjust your behaviours as necessary.

☑ Write down three ways you could use this strategy:

1. _____
2. _____
3. _____

☐ This strategy is a priority for me.
☐ I have implemented this strategy.

Understand Parkinson's Law

Parkinson's Law is the economic theory that provides that work expands to fill the time available for its completion.

You already know this to be true – if you have a month to complete a task, then it will take you a month to complete the task (because you will procrastinate a little, or jump in and out of the task without real focus, or spend time on rework, and then perfectionism or second guessing will creep in and the task suddenly becomes manifestly more complex than it ought to be).

Another way Parkinson's Law plays out is when, knowing you have a month to complete a task, you feel that you have plenty of time up your sleeve. And then, before you know it the month has passed and you haven't done the work, and you end up completing the task late into the night, the night before it is due, in an adrenalin-rushed frenzy.

You know you do this.

The solution? Don't give a task, any task, more time than it needs.

For typical tasks which you complete regularly, you should have a very good idea of how long these tasks generally take you – you can stress test this against your **time maps (31)**. For less typical tasks, estimate how long you think the task will take if you were working as productively as possible. Once you have these time estimates, lock the task into your **calendar (96)** (aka – set a **deadline (86)**). Continue to monitor how long tasks take and adjust your time estimates accordingly.

✎ Write down three ways you could use this strategy:

1. _____
2. _____
3. _____

☐ This strategy is a priority for me.
☐ I have implemented this strategy.

Set Realistic, Non-Negotiable Deadlines

A deadline is the time you set for completing a task or part of a task.

Referencing your **time maps (31)**, set realistic non-negotiable deadlines for each task to keep you on task and to minimise **time wastage (1)**. In terms of being realistic, this one is common sense:

- If a deadline is too short, you are setting yourself up for panic and failure.
- If the deadline is too generous, you are setting yourself up for procrastination and failure.

> ✍ Write down three ways you could use this strategy:
>
> 1. _____
> 2. _____
> 3. _____
>
> ☐ This strategy is a priority for me.
> ☐ I have implemented this strategy.

Leverage Parkinson's Law

Once you are actively setting and meeting **deadlines (86)**, challenge yourself to complete a given task in less time by leveraging Parkinson's Law. Start with the challenge to complete the task 10% faster – so a 10% time gain – then continue to tighten the screws until you reach the sweet point of maximum productivity: the best possible result in the shortest amount of time. Lock this time in as your new **deadline (86)** .

'Generally it would take 38 minutes to do a report, so we challenged our doctors to do a report in 36 minutes.'
Sunita Maheshwari, Chief Dreamer and Loop Closer, Teleradiology Solutions

'When there is a deadline you step into action to meet it. Business is a game – it has a start time and finish time and whoever has the highest score at the end of the game wins – deadlines need to be created to produce the tension necessary for performance.'
Tim Dwyer, Managing Director of Shirlaws Australia; Partner of BoB (Business of Brand) Group; creator of the Growth Metrics Program

---

☑ Write down three ways you could use this strategy:

1. _____
2. _____
3. _____

☐ This strategy is a priority for me.
☐ I have implemented this strategy.

Set A Timer

When you are working hard against a **deadline (86)**, do not watch the clock – this is a constant distraction which means you are **multitasking (120)** and not 100% focused on the task at hand. And that's bad for productivity.

For **single-focused (120)** work (without interruptions, email scanning, taking calls, procrastination or allowing other distractions), try setting an alarm for the amount of time you have allocated to the task. When the alarm goes off, regardless of whether you have completed the task or not, set it aside and **take a break (110)** .

This technique is known as the Pomodoro Technique, which encourages the use of a physical, wind-up, ticking alarm to make the experience of **single focusing (120)** more tangible and to aid absolute focus.

☑ Write down three ways you could use this strategy:

1. _____
2. _____
3. _____

☐ This strategy is a priority for me.
☐ I have implemented this strategy.

Break It Down With Mind Maps

Some tasks are more in the nature of big projects. Unless you have great project-management skills, large projects can be daunting when it comes to deciding where and how best to invest your time.

This is where mind mapping comes in.

Physically map out (on a whiteboard or butchers' paper, or in a mind mapping app) your big-picture goals and then break them down into small, bite-sized pieces. This will help avoid being overwhelmed by the sheer size of the project and the associated procrastination of not knowing where to start.

Transcribe the mind mapped outcomes into your **to-do list (92)**, allocate a **deadline (86)** to each small task, and lock each deadline into your **calendar (96)**. Allocating a deadline to each small task will provide you with an ongoing sense of momentum towards achieving the bigger project.

☑ Write down three ways you could use this strategy:

1. _____
2. _____
3. _____

☐ This strategy is a priority for me.
☐ I have implemented this strategy.

Plan

You have an overarching written **business plan (16)**, but you also need to plan out your year, month, week and each day. Your **to-do list (92)** used in conjunction with your **calendar (96)** are very powerful **time investment (2)** tools. Plan at least a week ahead to ensure you maintain a **proactive rather than a reactive mindset (91)**.

'When I plan ahead and batch my time in my diary in advance, I have a far greater chance of achieving my tasks than when I wing it.'

Jason Cunningham, Co-Founder, The Practice, and Media Personality

> ☑ Write down three ways you could use this strategy:
>
> 1. _____
> 2. _____
> 3. _____
>
> ☐ This strategy is a priority for me.
> ☐ I have implemented this strategy.

Active Vs Reactive Mindset

It is your business – so control the agenda.

You have set your **plan (90)**, so now be personally accountable to that plan. **Control (34)** what you do; when you do it; how long you spend on it; when you take calls; when you make calls; when you get on email; when you get off email; when you strategise; when you deliver; when you think; when you work in the back-end; when you are customer-facing; when you just do.

As soon as you deviate from your **plan (90)** by allowing **interruptions (124)**, by constantly jumping in and out of emails, by being a slave to your phone, or by allowing people or circumstances to distract you from your plan, you just lost control of the agenda.

Embrace an active rather than a reactive mindset.

'Maintaining control in your business is exactly the same as maintaining control as an elite athlete.

'The closer you get to the Paralympic cycle the crazier it becomes but also the more important it becomes to manage your time.

In that final part of the build up where everything is crazy and extreme, that's when you need to be saying No to a lot of it and just focus on what is core – the stuff that's going to affect the result at the end of the day.

'If what we are doing does not have a direct impact on the result then it becomes a second-level priority – because that stuff is just noise.

'It's all about control. It's very easy for me to decide what is affecting the result and what isn't and be able to say No to the other stuff.'

Brant Garvey, Paralympian and Motivational Speaker

☑ Write down three ways you could use this strategy:

1. _____

2. _____

3. _____

☐ This strategy is a priority for me.

☐ I have implemented this strategy.

To-Do Lists

If you have been subsisting with a mental to-do list to date then you are definitely not operating with maximum clarity over your priorities. The major problems with a mental to-do list are:

• You risk forgetting tasks.

- You limit your ability to accurately weigh up the competing value of multiple tasks, which in turn impacts your ability to set the right order of priority for your tasks.

- You risk letting procrastination take over, or putting particular tasks off unnecessarily, or allowing interruptions to distract yourself, or generating a growing too-hard basket.

- You risk **multitasking (120)** with the idea that you will get more done if you do more than one thing at a time.

A to-do list is a transcribed (handwritten or electronic) list of every task you need or want to complete in the short, medium and long term. Always include medium and long-term deliverables so that you can invest your time productively, and avoid a mad scramble as the deliverable date approaches.

I prefer a handwritten list because the act of transcribing a list by hand makes the **decision-making process (65)** around prioritising your to-do list much more tangible. A transcribed to-do list has other benefits, including:

1. It forces you to think about your tasks as **goals (15)**.

2. It requires you to articulate your goals or tasks in a succinct, action-oriented way.

3. It **frees up your mind (62)** for other thoughts, including how you are going to tackle the tasks.

Never underestimate the value of a SMART to-do list. You can access the free Time Stylers' SMART to-do list template at www. timestylers.com/resources/.

'I started every day writing down the three things I wanted to get done, and actually it was amazing how hard it was to get through

those three things! So I do think recognising, and it's taken me a long time to figure that out, that you don't have as much time as you think you have is crucial.'

Joy Foster, Founder and Managing Director, Tech Pixies

☑ Write down three ways you could use this strategy:

1. _____
2. _____
3. _____

☐ This strategy is a priority for me.
☐ I have implemented this strategy.

SMART To-Do List Process

Prior to prioritising your **to-do list (92)**, you need a simple **process (27)** to ensure you set your to-do list up for maximum success:

1. Once a week (either a Sunday night or a Monday morning) spend 10 minutes creating your master to-do list – a brain dump of every task you need to complete in the coming week.

2. Include tasks which are work; home; and life related. It makes sense to operate all tasks from one to-do list, otherwise you are left juggling multiple lists and trying to cross reference too many different priorities (and that is a complete **waste of your time (1)**).

3. Include in your master to-do list any tasks you need to keep an eye on to ensure you meet a **deadline (86)** in the next few

weeks or months, so that you are not caught out by a task you knew was looming but just didn't lock in a reasonable deadline to address.

4. Identify your top two or three most important tasks to complete on Monday (your ' **key tasks (94)** ').

5. Estimate how long you think your key tasks will take (refer to your **time maps (31)**). It is important that you allocate an appropriate and realistic time estimate to each task, otherwise your day could be thrown out by a task you have significantly underestimated and you will find yourself playing catch-up.

6. Lock a deadline (refer to your time estimates) into your **calendar (96)** for Monday to complete your two or three key tasks. The best time to perform your key tasks, and hence when you should lock in the deadline, is when you are at your best (during a **high-energy batch (102)**).

7. Each evening spend 10 minutes revisiting your master to-do list for the next day to identify:

- any new tasks which need to be accommodated
- your two or three key tasks for the next day
- if your time estimates are accurate (if they aren't, consciously adjust them)
- any long-term deliverables that require deadlines to be locked into your calendar
- completed tasks that can be crossed off your to-do list (this is the best bit).

8. Lock a deadline into your calendar for tomorrow night to start your master to-do list, and then a 10-minute deadline each night after that to update your to-do list – this will keep you

accountable until managing and maintaining your to-do list becomes a habit.

☑ Write down three ways you could use this strategy:

1. _____
2. _____
3. _____

☐ This strategy is a priority for me.
☐ I have implemented this strategy.

How To Identify Your Key Tasks

You have a lot on your plate – and a lot of competing demands from multiple sources. Sometimes it can feel incredibly overwhelming. So, how do you best decide what tasks take priority?

The Five Time Investment Basics for Setting Your Task Priorities are:

1. From your **to-do list (92)** first rank each task based on its **deadline (86)** – some deadlines will be determined by external factors such as customer demands and some deadlines will need to be imposed by you.

2. Elevate or rearrange any tasks which have a greater immediate impact on the bottom line of the business. For example, do you need to more immediately **focus (120)** on: sales; customer management; process efficiencies; marketing; website development?

3. The two or three tasks left at the top of your to-do list are your key tasks. Lock these into your **calendar (96)** for tomorrow.

4. Don't sweat on all of the other tasks at this stage – they are just white noise.

5. Imagine how productive you will feel, and how in control of your day, when you complete your two or three key tasks day in and day out.

☑ Write down three ways you could use this strategy:

1. _____
2. _____
3. _____

☐ This strategy is a priority for me.
☐ I have implemented this strategy.

Emptying Your Too-Hard Basket

Keep an eye on the tasks that seem to permanently reside on your **to-do list (92)**. If they are mundane, process-driven tasks, allocate a **deadline (86)** and schedule them into your **calendar (96)** during a **low-energy batch (103)** (this will often be after lunch or in the afternoon). If a particular task is a more complex task that you are procrastinating over, raise its status to that of a **key task (94)**, schedule a deadline and lock it into your calendar this week during a **high-energy batch (102)**.

☑ Write down three ways you could use this strategy:

1. _____
2. _____
3. _____

☐ This strategy is a priority for me.
☐ I have implemented this strategy.

Calendar Basics

Do not run multiple calendars (for example, work, personal and family). Not only are you **wasting your time (1)** juggling and cross referencing your multiple commitments across the different facets of your life, but there are simply too many moving parts to allow you to use all of your time well. Simple is best.

Commit to running all of your **key tasks (94)** (both work and home) from one calendar so that your calendar operates as a true reflection of your total time commitment. By having everything in one place you will maximise **control (34)** over your time and nothing is likely to fall through the cracks.

Once you have identified your key tasks from your **to-do list (92)** and have allocated **deadlines (86)**, lock these into your calendar immediately. This gives you an overarching view of your day, week, month and year, as well as the time available for other tasks from your to-do list (including your Wants).

Include all relevant information in the calendar entry, including contact details, and attach relevant documents. This way you won't waste 10 minutes at a later time trawling through your inbox looking for these details.

The disciplined use of your calendar will reduce the chances of procrastination; forgetting a task or a commitment; trying to be in two or more places at once; and will help you **reject (52)** distractions or **interruptions (124)**. Moreover, **batching (100)** each key task will help you **single focus (120)** (that is, reject **multitasking (120)**), allowing you to work more productively and move on to the next scheduled task with less wasted time.

☑ Write down three ways you could use this strategy:

1. _____

2. _____

3. _____

☐ This strategy is a priority for me.
☐ I have implemented this strategy.

Colour Code Your Calendar

Colour code different types of **batches (100)** in your **calendar (96)** so that you, and your team, can see at a glance how your day, week, month, and year are structured. Seeing your time in colour makes it very easy for you to see where you are spending your time.

SMART TIME INVESTMENT FOR BUSINESS

> **Tim Dwyer, Managing Director of Shirlaws Australia; Partner of BoB (Business of Brand) Group; creator of the Growth Metrics Program**

Tim Dwyer specialises in helping businesses strategically grow their assets, increase their business value, and hone and leverage their capabilities. He is the creator of the Growth Metrics Program which enables businesses to build more capability into their offering, ensuring business growth, increased value and profitability:

In Growth Metrics we use a colour-coding system called Colour My World, to integrate all of the elements of your life. It's all about getting stuff done and removing non-productive tasks from your day.

We have six colours which symbolise different types of tasks or activities that you need to spend time on in both your business and your personal life: Future Growth (Black); Today's Growth (Blue); Infrastructure (Red); Relationships (Green); Wealth (Purple); and Health (Orange).

An example of these categories is shown in the following table.

Category/ colour	Definition	Business sector (examples)	Family sector (examples)
Future Growth (Black)	Future growth and value-generating activities	• Brand • New products • New channels	Bucket list experiences that create long-lasting memories
Today's Growth (Blue)	Today's tasks that create value (revenue and good will)	• Sales • Delivery	Family time

178

Category/ colour	Definition	Business sector (examples)	Family sector (examples)
Infrastructure (Red)	Business support: everything that costs your business or you money and does not make money	• Financials • Billing • Money management • Legal • Compliance	Family chores
Relationships (Green)	Culture: being conscious of how you build relationships and connections with others	How you relate to your team and how you show up	Relationship management: family and friends
Wealth (Purple)	How you are creating wealth	For the business, yourself and your team	• Family budget • Income • Portfolio management • Investment streams
Health (Orange)	How you remain healthy	• Team exercise • Team health checks	• Personal health • Medicals • Exercise

To keep on top of your life, it is key to proactively schedule all six colours into your calendar. Start with a macro schedule (an annual planner), then move to your micro schedule (weekly calendar) using batching, and colour code each batch so you can see at a glance how you are tracking.

Use the following order:

1. **Future Growth in the family sector:** *You have to start with your personal (family) life, not your business life, because we are here to create a healthy, wealthy and well-lived life. Black in the family sector is all about scheduling time to plan the big family experiences, those living memories that your kids are going to talk about for the rest of their lives.*

2. **Future Growth in the business sector:** *Schedule when you are going to sit down (with your team if you have one) to strategically plan out the future growth of the business. Business strategy should be held offsite and be somewhere fun – because the key is to create memories of when you made important business decisions.*

3. **Infrastructure:** *Schedule when and how you are going to deal with the Red in both your business and your home life. You want to systemise the Red, and then outsource it as quickly as possible. For example, on the home front you can outsource and hire a cook for a day to make you a month's worth of healthy meals that you can put in the freezer. Meal making is a key piece of home infrastructure – and it takes time and, for many, does not always drive value – so systemise and outsource it. Then when you do want to cook it's because you want to enjoy the experience of cooking.*

4. **Today's Growth:** *Schedule batches of time to work on delivery in your business to allow you to get into the flow of a task. The same goes for family and personal enjoyment time – it's better if it is batched rather than sporadic and reactionary.*

5. **Relationships (in your business and at home):** *These will be happening all of the time, but need to be regularly checked in on. Schedule time to ask: 'How are you?', 'How are we?', 'What's working or not working?' Always allowing time to check in on your relationships means that the relationship is valued and will result in better outcomes for all.*

6. **Wealth:** *Schedule in half a day once a month to review the financial performance of your business. This is where you check in on the fact that you are actually building an asset and not just a job. Also schedule in an hour once a month to review wealth on the home front to ensure you are always focused on creating and retaining your wealth. Few people have a personal focus in this area and as such don't end up creating real wealth.*

7. **Health:** *Schedule Health in at a recurring time each quarter so that it is always on your radar. Ensure you have a target and set deadlines.*

As a rule of thumb, if your business is from one to four people you want to be spending about 20% of your time a year (which is equivalent to one day a week) on Black; with 10% of your time (equivalent to half a day a week) on Red; 10% of your time on a mix of Green, Purple and Orange (equivalent to half a day a week); and 60% of your time on Blue. Orange needs to be a daily ritual.

As you move to a business of 12 of more people, you need to spend more of your time on Black (40%) and less on Blue. At 24 or more people, the vast majority of your time will be in the Black.

The problem I see is that often business owners spend too much time in the Red and not enough time in the Black and Blue. Or too much time in the Black and Red and not enough time in the Blue. It's all about bringing awareness to where you need to spend your time versus where you are currently spending your time.

☑ Write down three ways you could use this strategy:

1. _____
2. _____
3. _____

☐ This strategy is a priority for me.
☐ I have implemented this strategy.

Create An Annual Calendar

At the start of each calendar year or financial year set up an annual calendar on a one-page spreadsheet or a one-page physical annual planner, because you want to be able to see your year on a plate. Refer to **colour code your calendar (97)** and, as with all things calendar, think **batching (100)**.

Your annual calendar is not set in stone – you will continue to finesse and update it throughout the year. Print out each version and always have it with you on the go so that when opportunities arise you can **make decisions fast (66)** .

'It's all about forward planning, because where I often fall down is when I haven't planned things far enough in advance. And then I suddenly think: "Oh my God, it's my children's school holidays, or it's their assembly, or it's their performance", and I'm like: "Oh no, I have a meeting". And then I'm scrambling, trying to reschedule, and sometimes you can't.

'My son is doing his final year of school, so as soon as I got the final examination dates at the beginning of the year I blocked out my calendar – so I can drive him to school on the mornings of the exams and I can cook him a big breakfast, and then the night before all of his exams I blocked out the time in my diary so I'm at home revising with him. And I was able to do that because I did that in January.

'It was a very stress-free, easy decision to make because I had planned well ahead. But often we don't do that, certainly I don't do that. Had it suddenly dawned on me the month before that I should block out that time, it would have been a nightmare.'

Cathy Hayward, Founder and CEO, Magenta

Write down three ways you could use this strategy:

1. _____

2. _____

3. _____

☐ This strategy is a priority for me.
☐ I have implemented this strategy.

Use A Cloud Calendar

An online calendar accessible through the cloud is an awesome time-saving tool. Benefits include allowing you to:

• keep your calendar up to date across each of your devices
• share your calendar with your team (if you have one) and with your family so that nothing falls through the cracks
• receive reminders, notifications and updates when you are on the go.

It's critical that you understand and leverage the full functionality of your online calendar – this will not only save you time, it will change the way you work. The fastest way to do this is to tap into an expert – ask around your **posse (81)** to find an expert user who can take you through the features of your chosen calendar.

☑ Write down three ways you could use this strategy:

1. _____
2. _____
3. _____

☐ This strategy is a priority for me.
☐ I have implemented this strategy.

Batch Similar Tasks

Batching is the process of grouping like tasks together and then blocking out slabs of time in your **calendar (96)** to complete those tasks in one chunk of time. Batching allows you to have one longer, concentrated period of time allocated to dealing with tasks in bulk as opposed to jumping in and out of smaller, like tasks repeatedly throughout the day. Batching also enables a clean and structured **calendar (96)**, and hence day, as opposed to a hectic and disorganised one.

Batching like activities together in your calendar (and **colour coding (97)** them) allows you to operate *in the zone* for a longer period of time. This also gives you greater control over the time it takes you to transition from one batch of tasks to the next, reducing the margin for error that comes with jumping in and out of tasks.

☑ Write down three ways you could use this strategy:

1. _____

2. _____

3. _____

☐ This strategy is a priority for me.
☐ I have implemented this strategy.

Batch Your Energy

Most of us have a sense of whether we are a morning person, afternoon person or a night owl. We generally know the time of day when we are at our best, have more energy than the norm, and when our brain is really firing. Equally, we generally know the time of day when we are at our lowest energy ebb.

Be aware of your energy levels when you map your time in your **time maps (31)** – this will allow you to match the type of task you should be performing to the level of energy you have at any given time.

Your **best time (102)** is your daily high-energy point (when you are at your most creative, enthusiastic and impactful). This time is sacred. It must be respected and only ever devoted to your best work – your most strategically important and **key task (94)** which will return the highest results for your business.

Never use your best time for anything less than your best and most important work.

Equally, your worst time is your daily **lowest energy ebb (103)**. This time should never be used for your best work – what a **waste of time (1)**. It will take you longer, will return a substandard result, and you will end up redoing the work at a time when your brain is actually working. Instead, use your worst time for your process-driven tasks – the tasks you can do with your eyes closed because they do not require your best brain. These are tasks that need to be done, just not at your best time.

Being conscious of your energy and working in this way will allow you to maximise your time, all of the time.

Use your time maps across a week to identify exactly when, during the morning, afternoon or evening, you are at your absolute best (and worst) and **batch (100)** tasks accordingly.

'I plan my day between 5 am and 7 am – the work is done then. Once I hit the office there is no time to be creative.'
Maria Hatzistefanis, President/CEO, Rodial Group (Rodial, NIP+FAB)

'I get my most focused work done late morning, after I have prayed, meditated and then done some sort of physical activity.

I like to work after a light breakfast; I find that my mind feels fresh and my body energised to focus properly.'
June Sarpong, MBE

☑ Write down three ways you could use this strategy:

1. _____
2. _____
3. _____

☐ This strategy is a priority for me.
☐ I have implemented this strategy.

Batch Your High Energy

You already know that it's important to invest your energy – each day you will cycle through periods of heightened focus, productivity and energy. You want to make the most of your high-energy periods by **batching (101)** this time for your best work.

From your **time maps (31)** you now know the time of the day that is your best time.

In your **calendar (96)**, batch 40 to 45 minutes of your best time for your first **key task (94)** as identified from your **to-do list (92)**. Don't **waste your best time (1)** on anything less than your best work.

For example, if you are a dynamo early in the morning, you will be full of energy at 6 am and ready to jump into the day. Don't waste this time on checking emails, reading the paper or killing time pottering around until the kids wake up. Instead, batch your best time into your calendar to deal with your hardest or most important key task for the day, the task that is complicated or requires uninterrupted and focused thinking.

Great uses of your best time include business planning, goal setting, strategic thinking, report writing, and client pitches.

> ☑ Write down three ways you could use this strategy:
>
> 1. _____
> 2. _____
> 3. _____
>
> ☐ This strategy is a priority for me.
> ☐ I have implemented this strategy.

Batch Your Low Energy

Identify from your **time maps (31)** the periods of your day when you are typically at your lowest energy ebb. **Batch (101)** this time in your **calendar (96)** for the more mundane, low-risk, process-driven work that does not require as much energy, brain power, concentration or thought.

Great uses of your worst time include approving invoices, paying bills, uploading business receipts, returning phone calls, staff one-on-one meetings and so forth.

Write down three ways you could use this strategy:

1. _____
2. _____
3. _____

☐ This strategy is a priority for me.
☐ I have implemented this strategy.

Batch A Buffer

A useful batching strategy is to factor a 30- to 60-minute buffer into your **calendar (96)** to allow for the unexpected. Not every day will run to plan, so it makes sense to factor into each day the possibility that you may need to dedicate time to something unforeseen. If nothing unexpected arises – brilliant, you just reclaimed 30 to 60 minutes to use for a want or you can move onto your next Must. If something unexpected does come up, you can shuffle your commitments knowing that you have a pre-batched buffer to play with.

Write down three ways you could use this strategy:

1. _____
2. _____
3. _____

☐ This strategy is a priority for me.
☐ I have implemented this strategy.

Control Your Device Usage

Where's your phone? Are you on it right now? I bet it's within arm's reach.

Your mobile phone is an essential business tool which can significantly reduce the amount of time many work tasks would otherwise take. However, your device also has the potential to cause a massive **waste of your time (1)** . On average, smartphone users:

- check their device 85 times (and for a total of over four hours) a day

- spend around 30% of their time each week on emails

- check their emails prior to starting the work day (80% of users)

- check their emails while on holiday (50% of users).

The constant compulsion to check your device coupled with using your phone as a *time killer* (think social media apps and news apps) can severely impact your ability to use all of your time well. Moreover, the proliferation of portable devices affords you constant exposure to this stream of information which, unchecked, allows for incessant **interruptions (124)** , decreased productivity and loss of focus.

In addition, when you start your day on your device and then continue to glance and review emails and text messages regularly throughout the day, all day, you are driving a **reactive rather than a proactive (91)** agenda – none of those messages or emails are going to be wishing you a great day. They are going to include words and phrases like: *I want... ; I need... ; When can you... ; Urgent...*

And guess what? You just lost control of your agenda.

On the flip side – if the vast majority of your interactions on your device are business related, then great work. After all, chances are that your target clients are also spending over four hours (and 85 touch points) on their phone a day too.

Think about your personal device habits: is the majority of your device usage adding value to your business or is it just a dopamine hit?

If you want to regain significant **control (34)** of your time, you need to instil some **boundaries (26)** around your device usage. Reflect on your own device usage. Don't just estimate the amount of time you spend on your devices – you want the hard data. You can see exactly how much time you spend from your **time maps (31)** . Mostly it will be a lot of random checks and glances – add them all up. You might be in for a shock.

☑ Write down three ways you could use this strategy:

1. _____
2. _____
3. _____

☐ This strategy is a priority for me.
☐ I have implemented this strategy.

Batch Emails

Batch (100) the time you will access your computer and other devices to read and write emails to maximise control (34) of your day. Depending on how much of your business delivery is driven from your inbox, you want to schedule two to four email batches a day. If your business delivery is heavily reliant on emails then you will look for more than four batches a day. Email batches should be around 30 to 45 minutes long.

Schedule your first email batch for the block of time immediately after the break (110) you take after your first key task (94) .

Between each email batch, turn your alerts off (visual and auditory) so that you aren't distracted or tempted to multitask (120) . Or better yet, put your device in another room.

If you find your early morning device addiction (either in terms of access to emails or social media (107)) hard to break, don't give up! Rather, employ the above technique with a one day on/one day off approach. For the day that you are 'off' (that is, not following the strategy), monitor the incoming traffic and assess how many genuinely urgent alerts you receive. Consider also whether your business could have been compromised by the hour's delay of dealing with your first key task (94) before you hit your device (and potentially became distracted).

As a general rule of thumb, unless you are a first responder (police, paramedic, doctor, firefighter) then an hour away from your device isn't likely to be life threatening.

☑ Write down three ways you could use this strategy:

1. _____
2. _____
3. _____

☐ This strategy is a priority for me.
☐ I have implemented this strategy.

'Your inbox is just a list of someone else's priorities. No-one is putting rockets into space if they are lost in their inbox.'
Glen Carlson, Co-Founder, Dent Global

'I'm kind of doing my thing and then I'll clock in and watch emails; and then I'm doing my thing and then I'll clock in and watch emails. We watch emails, I'm being foreign – I read emails even. I just don't have time to not spend my time wisely. I need to work on this habit!'
Geeta Sidhu-Robb, CEO, Nosh Detox

'Emails are my biggest sin. I can hang out in email all day long and find things to do. And it makes you feel good, but it's just "busy" work.

'I am aware of it and I have put lots of strategies in place to deal with it. I have streamlined all my comms into phone, text and email. I don't answer anything else. I just eschewed all of that noise. I don't take voicemail. I have put boundaries in place.

'Otherwise the "busy" work gets multiplied by 10, and before you know it you have spent five hours answering communications that are pretty much for the benefit of everyone else and not for you.

'When you wake up with a clear head, the worst thing you can do is fill it straight away with everybody else's noise from your inbox.'
Alexandra Depledge, Founder and CEO, Resi

Batch Social Media

Everything in **Batch Emails (106)** also applies to the constant and regular use of your device or computer to check your social media apps and news apps. Again – take control of your social media/news usage with **batching (100)** .

'My number one time management sin is Instagram. Do not open Instagram before you've done anything else that's pressing and that you need to do because you could get lost in a hole. And I think that's actually just a habit thing – and oftentimes I can tell myself that I'm doing it for a variety of reasons but it's a habit. That's probably my biggest sin.'
Michelle Kennedy, Co-Founder and CEO, Peanut

'One of the first things I did after I sold Hassle was to delete all social media apps from my phone.'
Alexandra Depledge, Founder and CEO, Resi

'I try hard to batch my social media use. Sometimes I do end up going down a rabbit hole and it's frustrating. I have time set aside for social media and I have a social media plan for the content. It's not easy, because social media is so distracting.

'I think it's important to ask yourself: "What am I using this platform for?" If you can't answer that question strategically then don't waste your time. I also think it is important to focus on one key platform – for me that's LinkedIn.'

Chris Robb, Founder and CEO, Mass Participation Asia

☑ Write down three ways you could use this strategy:

1. _____

2. _____

3. _____

☐ This strategy is a priority for me.
☐ I have implemented this strategy.

Batch Some More

Once you have the hang of batching, you will start to see batching opportunities everywhere. It becomes addictive. You can batch for:

- strategic planning
- delivery
- administration
- client meetings
- supplier meetings
- team or one-on-one meetings
- sales calls

- relationship management calls
- learning and continual professional development
- regulatory and compliance tasks
- invoicing
- bill paying
- tax management
- your Wants (exercise, hobbies, friends, family, lifestyle)
- home-based tasks (cleaning, bill paying, shopping, errands, cooking).

✐ Write down three ways you could use this strategy:

1. _____
2. _____
3. _____

☐ This strategy is a priority for me.
☐ I have implemented this strategy.

An Hour Of Power

Regardless of how good you are, or get, at investing your time, sometimes your back will just be against the wall with a crucial deliverable. It happens to all of us, no matter how well prepared we are.

When this happens, lock in an hour of power. Set your **timer (88)** for 60 minutes, eschew all **interruptions (124)** (close emails, turn off your phone, take yourself away from the general hubbub) and put your arse down and work. When the alarm goes off, take a 10-minute **break (110)** to give your brain a rest, and then repeat until you are done.

This intense level of work and focus is not sustainable long term, but used when absolutely needed, an hour of power will help you smash though your deliverables.

☑ Write down three ways you could use this strategy:

1. _____
2. _____
3. _____

☐ This strategy is a priority for me.
☐ I have implemented this strategy.

Take A Break

Take a break between each **batch (100)** of concentrated, **single-focused (120)** work. Your brain is not designed to work continuously without rest and recovery. Your brain is a massive user of energy – consuming about 20% of the body's calories – and this energy needs to be replenished and your brain needs to be rested.

Current research indicates that the best type of break is where you completely shift your focus from the task at hand to a short activity that boosts positive emotions: meditation; a walk; sitting in the sun or under a tree; daydreaming.

If your schedule doesn't allow regular breaks at a regular time, seize a short break where and when you can. Stepping away from a task for even two or three minutes will improve your productivity and decrease your error rate.

☑ Write down three ways you could use this strategy:

1. _____
2. _____
3. _____

☐ This strategy is a priority for me.
☐ I have implemented this strategy.

Triage Your Emails

Each time you undertake an **email batch (106)**, you will save a significant amount of time by spending the first five minutes of the batch triaging your inbox. The act of triaging is to simply make an assessment of the order of priority in which each email should be addressed.

The Seven Time Investment Basics for Triaging Your Emails are:

1. A simple and very effective email triaging strategy is the 4Ds. Create four new folders in your inbox: Deal With It; Delegate It; Delay It; Delete It (definitions below).

Email triage category	Action
Deal With It	Emails that are urgent.
	Emails that will take you five minutes or less to respond to.

Delegate It	Emails that can be dealt with by someone else (if you have a team).
Delay It	Emails requiring a considered response or some thinking time.
Delete It	Emails you can immediately delete, such as spam, junk or subscriptions you no longer want to receive (it is also a good strategy to unsubscribe from email posts you no longer wish to receive).

2. For the first five minutes of the email batch, quickly assess which folder to drag and drop each individual email. This is much easier to do if you (and your team, clients and suppliers) use **smart email subject lines (112)** .

3. Next, start working through the Deal With It folder.

4. If you complete this folder prior to the email batch ending, move on to the Delegate It folder and issue emailed instructions using the **SMART delegation (47)** strategy.

5. Next move on to the Delay It folder – use a template email to respond to the sender advising that you have their email and when you will come back to them by. It is polite to respond acknowledging receipt of the email, and it will also stop the sender chasing you up.

6. The Delete It folder is a favourite – drag, drop and forget.

7. As soon as the email batch is over, close your emails and **take a break (110)** . Keep your emails closed until your next email batch and then repeat this process from step 2 onwards.

If you currently have, or are about to engage, a virtual assistant or executive assistant (**outsource at work (39)**)) you can outsource or delegate to them the task of triaging your emails first thing each day; for example:

- general triaging
- attending to all emails within their remit
- forwarding or delegating emails to others within your team who are best placed to deal with the matter
- preparing draft responses to emails for your review
- developing email templates, auto-signatures and auto-responders to save time.

'I skim-read emails regularly throughout the day but, unless urgent, I save the ones that need answers and some thought until my train commute home.'

Claire Davenport, CEO, HelloFresh UK

☑ Write down three ways you could use this strategy:

1. _____

2. _____

3. _____

☐ This strategy is a priority for me.
☐ I have implemented this strategy.

Use Action-Led Email Subjects

Use action-led email subject lines to make it easier for the recipient to manage their email traffic. Educate your team, clients and suppliers to do the same – they will thank you, as this will make it easier for you all to **triage your emails (111)**.

Action-led subject lines make the act of triaging your emails significantly faster because you will not have to open each email to determine which of the 4Ds the email falls into. Using simple and consistent email subject lines will also help the recipient quickly triage their emails. For example:

Subject line	Description	Example
FYI:	Where non-urgent information is provided and no action is required	FYI: Product Launch Plan
URGENT FYI:	Where urgent information is provided and no action is required	URGENT FYI: Meeting Cancelled
Action:	Where non-urgent action is required	Action: Response to product plan launch required by [date]

Always pick up the phone or try to see the person face-to-face in situations where an urgent response is required. If this is not possible, use this email subject line:

URGENT Action:	Where urgent action is required	URGENT Action: Finalise Partnership proposal by [time]

☑ Write down three ways you could use this strategy:

1. _____
2. _____
3. _____

☐ This strategy is a priority for me.
☐ I have implemented this strategy.

Control Your Calls

Unlike emails, phone calls require real-time, one-to-one interaction with another person and so can suck up a lot of time unless managed consciously.

Where possible, turn your phone off and then return calls during a **call/device batch (100)** – this way you will more effectively **single focus (120)** on the task at hand and increase your productivity considerably. When you are in a device batch, triage your calls in the same way as you **triage your emails (111)**.

If you absolutely need to leave your phone on and take incoming calls, try to minimise the amount of time you are on each call by taking **control (34)** of the conversation.

Consider these phone strategies to ensure you control your time:

1. If you are pushed for time, don't ask: '*Hi, how are you?*' – as this is an invitation for the person to actually tell you how they are. Instead, try: '*It's good to hear from you. How can I help you?*'

2. When you take or make a call, take control of the conversation by framing the amount of time you have available: '*Hi Peggy, it's Yohan. I have 10 minutes before my next meeting and I wanted to…*'

3. In all cases when you are talking with a caller, if their request, issue or question is a rambling laundry list, this is a **waste of your time (1)**. Politely interrupt with: '*I'm just walking into a meeting and my mind is focused on that. Do you mind sending me a brief email letting me know exactly how I can help and I will come back to you this afternoon?*'

☑ Write down three ways you could use this strategy:

1. _____
2. _____
3. _____

☐ This strategy is a priority for me.
☐ I have implemented this strategy.

Get Smart With Voicemail

Gain **control (34)** over the time you spend on phone calls by recording a smart voicemail which directs your callers to a communication channel that works best for you – for example: '*You have reached Wal. Sorry I missed your call. Please send me a text message letting me know exactly how I can help you and I will get back to you today either by phone, text or email.*'

☑ Write down three ways you could use this strategy:

1. _____
2. _____
3. _____

☐ This strategy is a priority for me.
☐ I have implemented this strategy.

Embrace Texting

Text is a terrific mode of communication – it forces succinct and straight-to-the-point communication; it can be read and responded to in places and spaces where you might not necessarily be able to make or take a call or read and respond to an email, and it speeds up your interactions and communications.

☑ Write down three ways you could use this strategy:

1. _____
2. _____
3. _____

☐ This strategy is a priority for me.
☐ I have implemented this strategy.

Leave Smart Messages

When you make a call and the person isn't available, respect their time and yours and set up your future exchange for a good **time investment (2)** by leaving a meaningful message. For example: '*Hi, it's Fred, I'm sorry I missed you. Can you please text me the location and time of our meeting next week? I am looking forward to seeing you then.*'

☑ Write down three ways you could use this strategy:

1. _____

2. _____

3. _____

☐ This strategy is a priority for me.
☐ I have implemented this strategy.

Use Your Lost Time

Everyone has lost time that they don't take full advantage of. By identifying and harnessing your lost time, not only will you get through many of the smaller tasks that litter up your **to-do list (92)**, but you will also maintain a high level of productivity by using all of your time well.

From your **time maps (31)** and by generally reflecting on how your days seem to pan out, you can see that periodically throughout the day there are small periods of unexpected or unplanned for down time. For example:

- a client may be 10 minutes late for a meeting (+10 minutes)
- a task to which you have allocated an hour may only take 45 minutes (+15 minutes)
- you may have a commute to and from your workplace or between clients (+X minutes).

All of this is lost time and all of it is up for grabs.

Your current (and soon to be past) approach to these small pockets of time might be: '*I don't have enough time to start something else, so I won't...*', and instead, you **waste (1)** a little time before the next task is scheduled to commence.

No more!

From now on, plan ahead so that you are always ready to use your lost time when it arises. Prepare a list of small tasks that you can immediately turn to when you find yourself with some lost time, and keep the list with you on the go. For example:

5-minute tasks	• Make a cup of tea • Grab some water • Get up and walk around
10-minute tasks	• Network: – Maintain a list of key people you want to stay in touch with but who you don't often reach out to for lack of time.

10-minute tasks (cont.)	– When you make a call, frame the conversation to manage both your and your contact's time: *'Hi Fox, I have been thinking about you and found I had 10 minutes to spare between meetings. How are you?'* • Dictate into your device the actions from the meeting you just attended • Email batch • Phone call batch • Meditate
15-minute tasks	• Write a blog post • Record a video blog
20-minute tasks	• Listen to a podcast • Listen to a chapter of an audio book • Take a walk or stretch • Book your next holiday • Plan your next date night • Call your mum

There is no rule to say you can't use your lost time to surf social media – but for mine, that's just a **waste of time (1)** .

☑ Write down three ways you could use this strategy:

1. _____

2. _____

3. _____

☐ This strategy is a priority for me.
☐ I have implemented this strategy.

Use Your Commute

Your commute is the perfect time to get productive.

If you are commuting by car, you can use this time for (hands-free) telephone meetings, or for learning something new – download some excellent business podcasts.

If you are commuting by public transport, use this time for:

* **mind-mapping (89)** projects
* strategic thinking
* writing your **to-do list (92)**
* reading
* listening to your podcasts.

The best commute of all is by plane – this is the one time you are completely inaccessible to the otherwise unrelenting onslaught of communications. Air travel offers you an unequal opportunity to get a hell of a lot of work done with minimal interruption or to simply think, rest and recharge – embrace it.

> *'I am learning Mandarin and do my "lesson" in the car on the way to the office while I'm feeling alert.*
>
> *'I don't get a huge amount of downtime with emails starting at 7 am and Wechat (a Chinese communication app) going on until 10 pm some nights, so I generally use flying time to reflect and forward plan. It's during those hours that my creativity can flow and solutions to challenges are often found.'*
>
> **Catherine Cervasio**, Director, ALUXE Pty Ltd

'I travel a lot for work and am usually on planes, trains and taxis. I don't like to work during my commutes, I like to relax and use the time to think.'

June Sarpong, MBE

'My train commute is just over an hour each way. I use this time on the way home to answer the non-urgent emails I parked during the day, those emails that require some thought.'

Claire Davenport, CEO, HelloFresh UK

'I love my travel and use it for a mix of reading, thinking time and catching up on movies.'

Chris Robb, Founder and CEO, Mass Participation Asia

☑ Write down three ways you could use this strategy:

1. _____
2. _____
3. _____

☐ This strategy is a priority for me.
☐ I have implemented this strategy.

Control Meetings

If meetings seem to be taking over your working life, it's time to **take back control (34)** .

The Five Time Investment Basics of Meeting Management are:

1. Don't invite (or be) a spectator – meetings are for decision makers. If this is not you, politely decline.

2. Always have an agenda – the quickest way to waste time is a meeting without a list of topics for discussion. A short agenda is a good one – it makes for a quick meeting.

3. Keep minuting simple and action-based: *what* (what is the action?); *when* (when is the action due?); and *who* (who will take the action?).

4. Shake it up – standing meetings will result in a quick meeting; walking meetings allow you to get some exercise and fresh air at the same time; and online meetings avoid the commute, reduce emissions and save you loads of time.

5. Have a meeting budget: allocate a maximum amount of time per week to internal (non-revenue-generating) meetings and stick to it. If you need to exceed it, then remove something else from the meeting budget that week.

'We give people permission to walk out of meetings that are not productive. I came from a world where people went to meetings and everybody focused on the person who was speaking and we had notebooks and we didn't have laptops in front of us and we didn't fiddle with our thumbs, and I was quite rigid about that was how the world works. I've now learned the total opposite. I was totally wrong.'

Anne Boden, CEO and Founder, Starling Bank

☑ Write down three ways you could use this strategy:

1. _____

2. _____

3. _____

☐ This strategy is a priority for me.
☐ I have implemented this strategy.

Multitasking Versus Single Focus

Multitasking – the act of trying to force your brain to perform two or more tasks at the same time, usually with the assumption that you will get twice as much done – does not work.

In fact, the ability to successfully multitask is possessed by less than 2.5% of the human race. These individuals are so rare that they are called *super taskers*. For the rest of us mere mortals, multitasking is fundamentally a stop–start–stop–start–stop–start process of inefficiency. It costs you time, it is error generating, and ultimately it results in a poorer outcome and/or hours of rework.

For the data driven, multitasking will cost you as much as 40% of your productivity – which is the equivalent of losing a full night's sleep or dropping 10 IQ points.

Based on this, if you constantly multitask all day every day (for example, if you have your email alerts on all day and they constantly ping, vibrate or flash up on your device while you are not in an **email batch (106)**), then at best you are only ever working to 60% of your productive capacity. And that's not good enough.

Your best and only strategy to combat this complete **waste of time (1)** is to single focus on each discrete task. **Batch (100)** your tasks and **set a timer (88)** for each batch – this will significantly aid your ability to single focus.

> *'Sometimes I try to do too many things at one time. Rather than thinking: "Well I'll just do this for five minutes and then I'll do that task and then I'll do the next task", I'm trying to do bits of them all at the same time and therefore it takes much longer. And nothing is quite as good as it would have been if I had just focused on one thing at a time. On better days I sit down, and I'm a big list maker, and I'm like: "Right now I'm going to work through these things one at a time and that's how it's going to be", and then life is so much easier.'*
>
> **Cathy Hayward**, Founder and CEO, Magenta

☑ Write down three ways you could use this strategy:

1. _____
2. _____
3. _____

☐ This strategy is a priority for me.
☐ I have implemented this strategy.

Multitasking At Home

If you can cook the spaghetti bolognese while doing the dishes while vacuuming the floor while running the bath while feeding the pets while…knock yourself out. Yes, this is multitasking, however it is essentially just a juggle of a number of very simple, process-driven tasks that do not require your complete, focused attention.

> ☑ Write down three ways you could use this strategy:
>
> 1. _____
> 2. _____
> 3. _____
>
> ☐ This strategy is a priority for me.
> ☐ I have implemented this strategy.

Slow Cook

Save a lot of time by using a slow cooker to make simple, healthy, hearty soups and stews. Where possible, make a double batch and freeze half for another night. Winner winner chicken dinner.

> ☑ Write down three ways you could use this strategy:
>
> 1. _____
> 2. _____
> 3. _____
>
> ☐ This strategy is a priority for me.
> ☐ I have implemented this strategy.

Switch On And Off

Remember the **boundaries (26)** you have set. When you are with your family you want to be present and genuinely with them. When you are working on your business you want to be present and genuinely in the work zone.

Do not **waste your time (1)** being in a head space that is half focused on both at the same time – that's **multitasking (120)** and it does your productivity no favours.

A simple strategy to ensure you maximise how present you are in each of your respective head spaces is to choose a symbolic landmark (a particular building, tree, statue, house…) roughly half way along your commute from home to your place of business. When you reach the landmark on your commute to work, mentally switch off from family and switch on to work. When you reach the landmark on your commute home, mentally switch off from work and switch on to home.

If you work from home, then make the landmark the door to your office.

> ☑ Write down three ways you could use this strategy:
>
> 1. _____
> 2. _____
> 3. _____
>
> ☐ This strategy is a priority for me.
> ☐ I have implemented this strategy.

Control Interruptions

We live in the Age of Information, which also means we live in the Age of Distraction. Our average attention span is eight seconds (less than the common goldfish, which is believed to have an attention span of nine seconds – who knew?).

Interruptions occur up to 10 times an hour (that's every three minutes), and while external interruptions (from clients, your team, suppliers, and so on) are high on the list of offenders, the number one biggest culprit, accounting for over 40% of all interruptions to your time, is – *you.*

And, once interrupted, this is just a sample of what happens to your brain:

* it takes up to 23 minutes for you to refocus to the point of focus you had at the time of the interruption

* after the interruption you don't generally return straight to the task at hand, taking on an average of two different tasks before returning to the original task

* you tend to work harder and faster to make up for lost time, which increases your error rate twofold, along with increasing your levels of stress and frustration

* your productivity goes down by up to 40% (because you are **multitasking (120)**).

The Five Time Investment Basics for Managing Interruptions are:

1. Map your time: refer to your **time maps (31)** to identify who and what is interrupting or distracting you (remember this will often be you) and what prompts the interruption. If it's

SMART TIME INVESTMENT FOR BUSINESS

someone else, a regular saboteur, have a polite conversation
about how this is impacting your ability to best invest your
time.

2. Refer to the strategies around your **to-do list (92)**,
   calendar (96), **deadlines (86)** and **batching (100)**: these
   strategies ensure you have a **plan (90)** for your day that will
   minimise your hunt for distractions and your tolerance of
   interruptions.

3. **Single focus (120)** on each task.

4. **Set a timer (88)** to keep you accountable.

5. Maintain and manage a **parking list (126)**.

☑ Write down three ways you could use this strategy:

1. _____

2. _____

3. _____

☐ This strategy is a priority for me.
☐ I have implemented this strategy.

---

*'Open plan offices are like the devil. Collaboration can happen
when it needs to happen. It doesn't need to happen all the time.'*
Alexandra Depledge, Founder and CEO, Resi

*'My boyfriend travels quite a bit and he leaves the house at
5:15 am, and so I get up then with him and see him off and then
I work from about 5:15 am to 7:15 am. And those two hours are
really productive because everybody is silent and sleeping and it's*

joyful and you can just crack through so much work in a single-tasking fashion.'

Cathy Hayward, Founder and CEO, Magenta

Allow Urgent Interruptions

Some interruptions will be of an urgent, drop-everything nature, requiring your immediate attention. When the genuinely urgent does arise, pause and take a few seconds to note down exactly where you are up to with the task at hand and what your last thought was – this will reduce the amount of time it takes for you to refocus on the task at hand when you are able to return to it.

✏️ Write down three ways you could use this strategy:

1. _____

2. _____

3. _____

☐ This strategy is a priority for me.
☐ I have implemented this strategy.

Create A Parking List

The vast majority of **interruptions (124)** do not require your immediate attention. And yet, more often than not – over 70% of the time – we allow an interruption to take priority over the task at hand. When you do this you are falling back into your old habit of being **reactive rather than proactive (91)** and you just lost control of your agenda.

You can overcome this by creating a parking list – a list of every random thought that pops into your head when you are **single focused (120)** on another task (a potential for self-sabotage) and every interruption that comes at you from a multitude of other sources.

If you have a team, encourage them to park their questions or issues on the parking list, so that the matter can be addressed later at a suitable time for you all.

Apart from assisting you to single focus and eliminate interruptions, keeping a written parking list means that you will never, ever lose all of those amazing (or not so amazing) little ideas and thoughts that pop into your head at any time of the day or night.

☑ Write down three ways you could use this strategy:

1. _____

2. _____

3. _____

☐ This strategy is a priority for me.
☐ I have implemented this strategy.

Own Your Success

Stop waiting for that tap on the shoulder and for someone to finally call you out for being an imposter. Stop doubting yourself. You did not get here by luck. No-one gift wrapped your business and handed it to you. You got here by talent, **grit (14)** and hard work.

Do not **waste your time (1)** by continually re-setting the bar so high. Set it just right, just out of reach, to give yourself something juicy to aim for.

And enjoy your success along the way.

Catherine Cervasio, Director, ALUXE Pty Ltd

Catherine Cervasio is the founder of Aromababy – the world's first skincare brand for mother and baby to combine the use of natural and organic ingredients with research, creating a new category in retail in 1994. An early adopter of the China opportunity, Aromababy was the first Australian product of its kind to be approved for retail sale in China. Catherine purposely scaled back her brand until 12 months ago, to focus on her family. She has recently resumed a growth strategy and participated in the first Australian all-female trade delegation to China as part of the Victorian Government's Women in International Business initiative. Catherine travels extensively to Asia for her business and also to provide workshops and education in the mother/baby sector – something she is very passionate about:

Success is different to everyone. It's important to know what it means for you. For me it's about balance, about family and lifestyle, about enjoying what I am doing while I'm creating income. It's more than just my business or my brand. We often measure our success by financial means or against other high-profile business people, however for me success is very individual – even private. It's about achieving your own goals, in your own time. I make no excuses for putting Aromababy on the back burner while raising two beautiful young men. I now have a 24-year-old brand that has stood the test of time because of the authenticity it has – my core values are at the heart of my business. Do I feel successful? Absolutely.

'It's so important to own your success – because if you don't someone else will.'

June Sarpong, MBE

'We recently launched an Un-Stereotyping product that detects whether or not ads are sexist, and we launched it on International Women's Day. Consumers are increasingly unhappy with the outdated gender stereotypes that pervade the media landscape. So, we launched a free, data-driven tool that helps brands look at their ads in a different light, identifying ads that perpetuate outdated gender stereotypes (for example, the harried housewife; the hapless dad), and giving them the data to decide whether and how they should recut the ad or better still reset the way in which they approach the representation of women in their advertising. That was a really exciting moment in the evolution of the business as we were using our technology and data to make a real difference in the world.

'Another amazing moment was being in the Guinness Book of World Records *with the most viewed ad of all time [Dove's 'Real Beauty Sketches', a moving film from Dove that was part of their Self-Esteem Project] – it was an awesome feeling to know that we were part of popular culture and at the same time using our distribution platform to drive a positive change in how women perceive themselves. Our vision has remained unchanged – to be the team and the tech that transforms advertising for the better.*

'Being an entrepreneur, there are ups and downs – it's a roller coaster – but there are some moments when you just say: "Yes, we've moved the dial – we are helping to transform our industry for the better." And those moments are really exciting and worth celebrating – they make the tears and the sweat worthwhile!'

Sarah Wood, Co-Founder and Chair, Unruly

'We're pretty much making it up every day as we go along. I don't think I've ever really known what I am doing. I think I've always just kind of used a bit of intuition and a bit of intelligence and a whole lot of grit to make things happen.

'I completely feel inadequate most of the time. I think most of us do, we just won't admit it. We're constantly moving that internal bar higher and higher and never reaching it.

'My mum was awesome about this. She said: "When you realise that when you walk into a room that everyone else is pretending, that is the minute you'll feel better."

Alexandra Depledge, Founder and CEO, Resi

☑ Write down three ways you could use this strategy:

1. _____
2. _____
3. _____

☐ This strategy is a priority for me.
☐ I have implemented this strategy.

Just Start

Sometimes a business opportunity will unexpectedly present itself, so be open to this.

More often than not, there is never going to be an absolutely perfect time to start your business or launch your new product or service. There will always be a reason why *now is not quite the right time*. You may think, or you may be told, that you need more time, or more money, or more data, or more investment, or more experience, or more opinions, or more ideas, or more people in your network, or more talent, or more passion.

Just start. Just make it happen – because the one thing you can never get more of is time. And every day you delay and make excuses is a day you lose.

Maria Hatzistefanis, President/CEO, Rodial Group (Rodial, NIP+FAB)

Maria Hatzistefanis was working in the financial services sector in New York – and hating it. She describes it this way:

222

*I was always interested in business and went to New York to study.
I didn't know what I wanted to do with my life and everyone was
going into banking so I thought: 'Okay, I will go into banking, that
sounds alright.' It was the nineties and that was the cool thing to do.*

*Within a couple of years I was hating it – everyone was reading the
Financial Times and I was reading Vogue – I didn't fit in there.*

*And this lack of interest and passion probably showed, and one day
I was called into the boardroom and I was fired then and there. I was
shattered – that was my first real job and it was a big shock.*

*But in hindsight this was the best thing that ever happened to me.
It made me think about what I wanted to do with my life, where
my passion lay, and I thought: 'I will start my own business – I love
beauty'.*

*I was always creative and there was nothing exciting in beauty.
I wanted to bring more fun into the skincare industry and products
that targeted specific concerns. At that point the beauty industry was
very basic, and I thought: 'It's not so hard, I will start my own brand.'*

*It was actually a blessing that I did not come from the beauty
industry – I was very naive and it helped me, because if I knew what
it was going to take, I don't think I would have started.*

*I had research skills from finance and I treated this as a project.
Coming up with a formula for the product was not the hard part
– very quickly, within six months I found a lab that I loved. The
packaging was also sorted quite quickly. The challenge for me was to
get the products into the stores.*

*There was one store I had in mind, a boutique store that was
experimenting with new brands. I showed the buyer my four products
and I said: 'I will do a lot of press for you, and I will tag you in the
press and I will be here every weekend to sell the products'. I think she*

felt sorry for me. She said: 'Okay, I will give you a shelf and you have six months to make it work'.

That was the first store. But going from that one store to my next store took a while.

'Don't worry – it is all going to happen the way it's going to happen. You just need to show up, open up and let the universe put air beneath your wings.'

Geeta Sidhu-Robb, CEO, Nosh Detox

'Be conscious of your timing: being too early is just as heinous a crime as being too late.'

Sarah Wood, CEO, Unruly

'I would have told my 18-year-old self to have more fun along the way. It can be very serious but if you work hard and have a little luck, you'll make it. Someone once said: "Jump and the net will be there." I believe that is true.'

Joy Foster, Founder and Managing Director, TechPixies

'I fell pregnant six weeks after we'd secured $6 million of funding, so the timing was horrendous. I started a family right at the point where we were expanding through Ireland, Germany and France, which was also pretty horrendous if I'm honest.

'But then again, I think our paths are what they are and I wouldn't change anything.

224

'When it's your own business you can't just say: I'm sorry gang, I'm taking six months out. *It doesn't work that way.'*

Alexandra Depledge, Founder and CEO, Resi

Sunita Maheshwari, Chief Dreamer and Loop Closer, Teleradiology Solutions

Doctors Sunita Maheshwari and her husband Arjun trained at Yale, but after living and working in America they were keen to return to India where the healthcare need was higher. Despite his training, Arjun could not secure a job in India because he was considered over-qualified. And so, for a period, he commuted between India and Yale where he continued to work as a radiologist. It was during a stint at work in Yale where the chairman mentioned the difficulty they were having in getting a nightshift radiologist at the local hospital. Arjun said that he could manage the role from India, given the nightshift in America was Arjun's day shift. At this point, Sunita and Arjun still intended to be doctors, not entrepreneurs:

There was no grand idea to have a business, it was just for Arjun to have a job. But then, there was a huge anti-outsourcing movement in the US and Yale closed the program. We had an idea that was too advanced for the way the market was thinking – it was too early, people were not comfortable.

But we knew it was a great idea so we decided to incorporate a company and put ourselves out there on the world wide web as providing teleradiology services. We started the business from our guest room. Before we knew it we had a company.

Teleradiology Solutions is now the largest teleradiology company in India, employing 500 staff and working with hospitals across India, the United States, Africa, Singapore and the Middle East.

'I did what everyone does when they have a good idea, which is I went back to work and I forgot about it and I just focused on doing something else.

'And so I suppose there was this turning point where I thought – if I don't do it now, I'm not going to do it and I'll continually be that *person who speaks with their friends about: "Wouldn't it be great if there was this platform?" And I'd been that for long enough and I think my friends were tiring of me. And so I decided to do it, and the starting premise was: can I use everything I know about dating and the algorithms that we know work for connecting people romantically – can we use that to connect women who are mothers?'*

Michelle Kennedy, Co-Founder and CEO, Peanut

'You don't have to have it all figured out. I like to take business one chunk at a time – a day, a week or a month. The important thing is to just keep moving forward.'

Catherine Cervasio, Director, ALUXE Pty Ltd

A Final Word

Time is your most precious resource – guard it jealously; leverage it; protect it; invest it with intent and always use it well.

Enjoy the ride – *Kate x*

Thank You

A very warm thank you to the following incredible business people who gave me their time, offered their invaluable business insights, and shared their stories:

June Sarpong
Tim Dwyer
Maria Hatzistefanis
Alexandra Depledge
Michelle Kennedy
Susan Burton
Anne Boden
Cathy Hayward
Andrea Loubier
Sarah Wood
Joy Foster
Brent Garvey

Devika Wood
Anu Acharya
Geeta Sidhu-Robb
Sunita Maheshwari
Glen Carlson
Hunter Leonard
Holly Tucker
Chris Robb
Jason Cunningham
Claire Davenport
Catherine Cervasio

About Kate Christie

Kate Christie, Founder and CEO of Time Stylers, is a time investment expert, global speaker and bestselling author.

Kate consults to big and small business, schools, government agencies, and C-suite executives on maximising individual time spend and managing organisational drag through SMART time investment strategies. She has appeared on television, radio and in print as a leading commentator on time management and maximising work/life integration to ensure success across work, family, community, and life.

SMART Time Investment for Business is Kate's third book. Her previous books are:

- *Me Time: The Professional Woman's Guide to finding 30 guilt-free hours a month*
- *SMART Time Management for Doctors*

With a reputation for helping her clients find 30 hours of lost time a month, Kate's focus is to ensure you are left educated, entertained and with a lasting impact on the way you choose to live, work and play.

Please connect with Kate at:

Mail: info@timestylers.com
Web: www.timestylers.com
LinkedIn: www.linkedin.com/in/kate-christie/
Facebook: www.facebook.com/kate.christie.92

About Time Stylers

Time Stylers was founded in 2014 by Kate Christie. Our purpose is to help you gain control of your time across your business, family, community, and life. The Time Stylers approach is to combine coaching, education and productivity strategies to create, build and sustain a much smarter personal and business time investment framework to help you free up hours of your precious time.

Everything we do is intelligently, strategically and enthusiastically focused on maximising your time so you can live the life you love.

The whole idea of *SMART Time Investment for Business* is to inform and educate you on how to better invest your time – to move you away from working in a highly reactive mode to working in a highly proactive mode. You now have well over 100 strategies to help you gain control of your time.

If you want to know more about how Time Stylers can work with you individually or with your business to help you achieve awesome results, check out our programs at www.timestylers.com or send an email to info@timestylers.com with your contact details and we can discuss coaching, workshop and education options with you. Our products include:

Free resources: Time Stylers has a range of fantastic free time investment templates, tools and resources (for both your business and home) which you can access at www.timestylers.com/resources/

Books: Purchase this book, and Kate's other books, at www.timestylers.com or on amazon.com and a range of other online bookstores, and work your way through the strategies using your own self-commitment and personal drive to achieve great results.

DIY 30-Day Time Transformation Program: A 30-day online program specifically designed to help business owners and entrepreneurs invest their time with intent for greater success. Content includes:

• Kate Christie's ebook: *The SMART Time Investment Workbook*

• Daily emails from Kate Christie for 30 days with instructions, advice, tips, implementation guidance and motivation

• Daily Vlogs from Kate Christie for 30 days

• Action Plan

• Tools and Templates

• Time Tracker

Personalised DIY: A mix of online and offline support. Personalised DIY gives you:

• Access to the 30-Day Time Transformation Program

• Access to the Time Stylers team to submit worksheets for evaluation

• 4 × 30-minute Skype/Zoom calls with a member of the Time Stylers' team to address particular time challenges you are stuck on

Business/Team Workshops: 2.5-hour bespoke SMART Time Investment Workshop tailored to the specific needs of your Business and Team and each individual in the team, including:

• Pre-workshop survey to identify key time investment challenges

- Guided pre-workshop individual time audit
- 2.5-hour workshop addressing the specific needs of your Business and Team
- All materials supplied
- A written report on survey data

1:1 Time Investment Coaching: 9-week bespoke face-to-face productivity and business coaching with Kate Christie. All materials supplied and results guaranteed.

Speaking, Events and Conferences: Kate Christie can be engaged to speak at your next national or international conference.

www.ingramcontent.com/pod-product-compliance
Lightning Source LLC
Chambersburg PA
CBHW060400220326
41598CB00023B/2979